COMMON CORE

MATH 4 Today

Daily Skill Practice

Grade 2

Erin McCarthy

Carson-Dellosa Publishing, LLC
Greensboro, North Carolina

Credits

Content Editor: Jennifer B. Stith

Copy Editor: Beatrice Allen

Visit *carsondellosa.com* for correlations to Common Core State, national, and Canadian provincial standards.

Carson-Dellosa Publishing, LLC
PO Box 35665
Greensboro, NC 27425 USA
carsondellosa.com

ISBN 978-1-62442-600-1

Table of Contents

Introduction

Common Core Math 4 Today: Daily Skill Practice is a perfect supplement to any classroom math curriculum. Students' math skills will grow as they work on numbers, operations, algebraic thinking, place value, measurement, data, and geometry.

This book covers 40 weeks of daily practice. Four math problems a day for four days a week will provide students with ample practice in math skills. A separate assessment of 10 questions is included for the fifth day of each week.

Various skills and concepts are reinforced throughout the book through activities that align to the Common Core State Standards. To view these standards, please see the Common Core State Standards Alignment Matrix on pages 7 and 8.

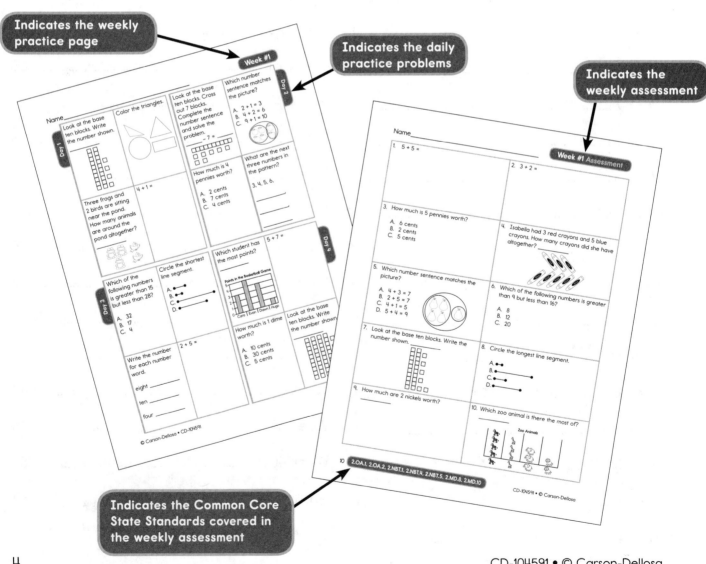

Indicates the weekly practice page

Indicates the daily practice problems

Indicates the weekly assessment

Indicates the Common Core State Standards covered in the weekly assessment

Incorporating the Standards for Mathematical Practice

The daily practice problems and weekly assessments in *Common Core Math 4 Today: Daily Skill Practice* help students achieve proficiency with the grade-level Common Core State Standards. Throughout the year, students should also work on building their comfort with the Standards for Mathematical Practice. Use the following suggestions to extend the problems in *Common Core Math 4 Today: Daily Skill Practice*.

1. **Make sense of problems and persevere in solving them.**

   Students should make sure that they understand a problem before trying to solve it. After solving, students should check their answers, often just by asking themselves if their answers make sense in the context of the question. Incorporate the following ideas into your Math 4 Today time:

   - Encourage students to underline the important parts of word problems and to draw lines through any extra information.
   - Allow students to talk through their answers with partners and explain why they think their answers make sense.

2. **Reason abstractly and quantitatively.**

   Students should be able to represent problems with numbers and symbols without losing the original meaning of the numbers and the symbols. A student who is successful at this practice will be able to reason about questions related to the original problem and use flexibility in solving problems. Incorporate the following ideas into your Math 4 Today time:

   - Ask students questions to extend the problems. For example, if a problem asks students to evenly divide a set of 10, ask them to describe what they would do if the set increased to 11.
   - Have students choose a computation problem and write a word problem to accompany it.

3. **Construct viable arguments and critique the reasoning of others.**

   Students should understand mathematical concepts well enough to be able to reason about and prove or disprove answers. As students become more comfortable with mathematical language, they should use math talk to explain their thinking. Incorporate the following ideas into your Math 4 Today time:

   - Have students work with partners and use mathematical language to explain their ways of thinking about a problem.
   - Encourage students to use manipulatives and drawings to support their reasoning.

4. **Model with mathematics.**

   Students should apply their mathematical knowledge to situations in the real world. They can use drawings, graphs, charts, and other tools to make sense of situations, as well as use skills such as estimation to approach a problem before solving it. Incorporate the following ideas into your Math 4 Today time:

- Encourage students to take a problem they have solved and explain how it could help them solve a problem in their own lives.
- Ask students to identify tools, such as charts or graphs, that could help them solve a problem.

5. **Use appropriate tools strategically.**

   Students should be able to use a range of tools to help them solve problems, as well as make decisions about which tools to use in different situations. Proficient students will use skills such as estimation to evaluate if the tools helped them solve the problem correctly. Incorporate the following ideas into your Math 4 Today time:

   - Ask students to discuss which tools would be most and least helpful in solving a problem.
   - As a class, discuss how two students using the same tool could have arrived at the same answer. Encourage students to identify the errors and the limitations in using certain tools.

6. **Attend to precision.**

   Students should be thorough in their use of mathematical symbols and labels. They should understand that without them, and without understanding their meanings, math problems are not as meaningful. Incorporate the following ideas into your Math 4 Today time:

   - Ask students to explain how a problem or an answer would change if a label on a graph were changed.
   - Have students go on a scavenger hunt for the week to identify units of measure in the problems, operations symbols, or graph labels.

7. **Look for and make use of structure.**

   Students identify and use patterns to help them extend their knowledge to new concepts. Understanding patterns and structure will also help students be flexible in their approaches to solving problems. Incorporate the following ideas into your Math 4 Today time:

   - Have students become pattern detectives and look for any patterns in each week's problems.
   - Ask students to substitute a different set of numbers into a problem and see if any patterns emerge.

8. **Look for and express regularity in repeated reasoning.**

   Students are able to use any patterns they notice to find shortcuts that help them solve other problems. They can observe a problem with an eye toward finding repetition, instead of straight computation. Incorporate the following ideas into your Math 4 Today time:

   - Allow students to share any shortcuts they may find during their problem solving. As a class, try to understand why the shortcuts work.
   - When students find patterns, have them explain how the patterns could help them solve other problems.

CD-104591 • © Carson-Dellosa

Common Core State Standards Alignment Matrix

STANDARD	W1	W2	W3	W4	W5	W6	W7	W8	W9	W10	W11	W12	W13	W14	W15	W16	W17	W18	W19	W20
2.OA.1	●	●	●	●	●	●	●	●	●	●	●	●	●	●	●	●	●	●	●	●
2.OA.2	●	●	●	●	●	●	●		●	●	●	●	●	●	●	●	●	●	●	●
2.OA.3		●		●		●	●		●	●	●	●	●	●	●	●			●	●
2.OA.4													●	●	●	●		●	●	●
2.NBT.1	●		●			●	●	●	●	●	●	●	●	●	●	●	●	●	●	●
2.NBT.2	●		●		●	●			●	●	●	●	●	●	●	●	●	●	●	●
2.NBT.3	●	●	●	●	●	●	●	●	●	●	●	●	●	●	●	●	●			●
2.NBT.4	●	●	●	●	●	●	●	●	●	●	●	●	●	●	●	●	●	●	●	
2.NBT.5	●	●	●					●	●	●	●	●	●	●	●	●	●	●	●	●
2.NBT.6																●	●		●	●
2.NBT.7																				
2.NBT.8		●	●	●		●	●	●			●	●				●	●	●		●
2.MD.1		●		●			●						●							
2.MD.4																				
2.MD.5																				
2.MD.6			●	●			●	●	●	●	●									
2.MD.7				●	●	●	●	●	●	●	●	●	●	●	●	●	●	●	●	●
2.MD.8	●	●	●	●	●	●	●	●	●	●	●	●	●	●	●	●	●	●	●	●
2.MD.9																				
2.MD.10	●	●	●	●	●	●	●	●	●	●	●	●								
2.G.1	●	●	●	●	●	●	●	●	●	●	●	●								
2.G.2													●							
2.G.3																				

W = Week

2.NBT.9, 2.MD.2, and 2.MD.3 are not included in this book. Various activities may be adapted to address them.

Common Core State Standards Alignment Matrix

STANDARD	W21	W22	W23	W24	W25	W26	W27	W28	W29	W30	W31	W32	W33	W34	W35	W36	W37	W38	W39	W40
2.OA.1	•	•	•	•	•	•	•	•	•	•	•	•	•	•	•	•	•	•	•	•
2.OA.2	•	•	•	•	•	•	•	•	•	•	•	•	•	•	•	•	•	•	•	•
2.OA.3	•				•		•		•		•		•		•			•		•
2.OA.4	•		•	•	•					•		•		•					•	
2.NBT.1	•				•	•		•			•	•		•			•	•	•	
2.NBT.2	•	•	•			•			•	•		•	•		•	•	•			•
2.NBT.3	•	•		•	•	•	•	•	•		•	•	•	•	•	•	•	•	•	•
2.NBT.4	•	•		•	•	•		•		•	•			•		•		•		•
2.NBT.5	•	•	•	•	•	•	•	•	•	•	•	•	•	•	•	•	•	•	•	•
2.NBT.6	•	•	•	•	•	•				•				•				•		
2.NBT.7		•	•	•	•	•	•	•	•	•	•	•	•	•	•	•	•	•	•	•
2.NBT.8					•			•	•	•		•			•	•			•	
2.MD.1			•	•	•	•	•	•	•	•	•		•		•	•			•	
2.MD.4		•	•	•	•	•	•	•	•	•										
2.MD.5		•	•	•	•	•	•	•		•				•			•			
2.MD.6		•	•	•		•	•	•	•											
2.MD.7	•	•	•	•	•	•	•	•	•	•	•	•	•	•	•	•	•	•	•	•
2.MD.8	•		•	•	•	•	•	•	•	•	•	•	•	•	•	•	•	•	•	•
2.MD.9											•	•	•	•	•	•	•	•	•	•
2.MD.10											•	•	•	•	•	•	•	•	•	•
2.G.1											•	•	•	•	•	•	•	•	•	•
2.G.2	•												•							
2.G.3											•	•	•	•	•	•	•	•	•	•

W = Week

2.NBT.9, 2.MD.2, and 2.MD.3 are not included in this book. Various activities may be adapted to address them.

CD-104591 • © Carson-Dellosa

Name_____

Day 1

Look at the base ten blocks. Write the number shown.

_____

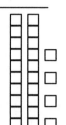

Color the triangles.

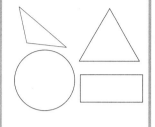

Day 2

Look at the base ten blocks. Cross out 7 blocks. Complete the number sentence and solve the problem.

_____ – 7 = _____

Which number sentence matches the picture?

A. 2 + 1 = 3
B. 4 + 2 = 6
C. 9 + 1 = 10

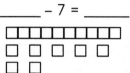

Three frogs and 2 birds are sitting near the pond. How many animals are around the pond altogether?

_____

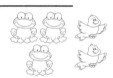

4 + 1 =

How much is 4 pennies worth?

A. 2 cents
B. 7 cents
C. 4 cents

What are the next three numbers in the pattern?

3, 4, 5, 6,

_____,

_____,

_____

Day 3

Which of the following numbers is greater than 15 but less than 28?

A. 32
B. 17
C. 4

Circle the shortest line segment.

A.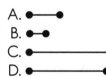
B.
C.
D.

Which student has the most points?

_____

Points in the Basketball Game

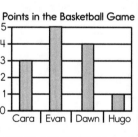

5 + 7 =

Day 4

Write the number for each number word.

eight _____

ten _____

four _____

2 + 5 =

How much is 1 dime worth?

A. 10 cents
B. 30 cents
C. 5 cents

Look at the base ten blocks. Write the number shown.

_____

Name_____

1. 5 + 5 =	2. 3 + 2 =

3. How much is 5 pennies worth?

    A. 6 cents
    B. 2 cents
    C. 5 cents

4. Isabella had 3 red crayons and 5 blue crayons. How many crayons did she have altogether? _____

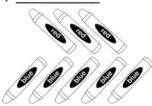

5. Which number sentence matches the picture?

    A. 4 + 3 = 7
    B. 2 + 5 = 7
    C. 4 + 1 = 5
    D. 5 + 4 = 9

6. Which of the following numbers is greater than 9 but less than 16?

    A. 8
    B. 12
    C. 20

7. Look at the base ten blocks. Write the number shown. _____

8. Circle the longest line segment.

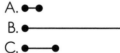

    A.
    B.
    C.
    D.

9. How much are 2 nickels worth?

_____

10. Which zoo animal is there the most of?

_____

Zoo Animals

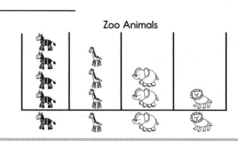

2.OA.1, 2.OA.2, 2.NBT.1, 2.NBT.4, 2.NBT.5, 2.MD.8, 2.MD.10

Name_____

Day 1

Look at the base ten blocks. Write the number shown.
_____

Color the circles.

Five squirrels were in a tree. Seven more squirrels came. How many squirrels were in the tree altogether? _____

3 + 4 =

Day 2

Look at the base ten blocks. Write the number shown.
_____

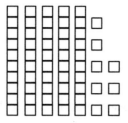

Which number sentence matches the picture?

A. 5 + 1 = 6
B. 3 + 3 = 7
C. 5 + 2 = 7

How much is 1 dime and 1 penny worth?

A. 20 cents
B. 11 cents
C. 6 cents

Is this number of rectangles even or odd? _____

Day 3

7, _____, _____, 10

Which numbers go on the blank lines?

A. 1 and 2
B. 6 and 5
C. 8 and 9

How long is the pencil? _____

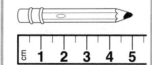

Write the number for each number word.

one _____

three _____

five _____

6 + 2 =

Day 4

Total Number of Erasers

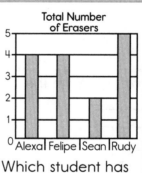

Which student has the least amount of erasers? _____

What is 10 more than 15?

_____

Write <, >, or = to make the statement true.

8 ⃝ 12

Dion has 1 dime and 1 nickel. How much money does he have?

A. 2 cents
B. 15 cents
C. 20 cents

Name_____

1. 6 + 5 =	2. 2 + 6 =

3. Is the number of bananas even or odd?

_____

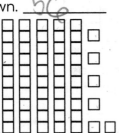

4. Which number sentence matches the picture?

A. 6 – 4 = 2
B. 6 + 4 = 10
C. 6 + 0 = 6

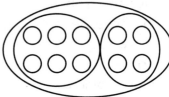

5. Write the number for each number word.

eleven _____

six _____

eight _____

6. Paige has 2 dimes and 3 pennies. How much money does she have?

A. 11 cents
B. 23 cents
C. 8 cents

7. Look at the base ten blocks. Write the number shown. __56__

8. Who has read more books than Beth?

_____

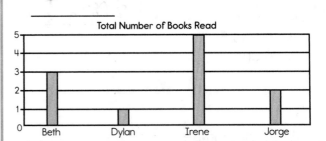

9. Color the circles.

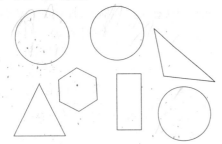

10. Write <, >, or = to make the statement true.

10 5

2.OA.2, 2.OA.3, 2.NBT.3, 2.NBT.4, 2.NBT.5, 2.MD.10, 2.G.1   CD-104591 • © Carson-Dellosa

Name_____

Day 1

Color the quadrilaterals.
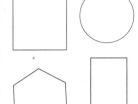

3 + 4 =

Draw base ten blocks to show 25.

Ten apples grew on a tree. Three apples fell off the tree. How many apples were left on the tree? _____

Day 2

Look at the base ten blocks. Write the number shown.

_____
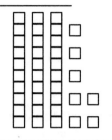

Which number sentence matches the picture?

A. 7 + 4 = 11
B. 5 − 3 = 2
C. 8 − 2 = 6

Victor had 2 nickels. Shelby gave him 2 pennies. How much money does Victor have now? _____

Is the number of circles even or odd? _____

Day 3

7 − 4 =

What number does the question mark represent?

_____
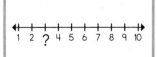

How long is the ladybug?

_____
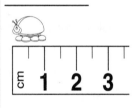

Which numbers are between 20 and 32?

A. 50 and 51
B. 30 and 31
C. 40 and 41

Day 4

Write the number that is 10 less than 68. _____

Write <, >, or = to make the statement true.

33 ◯ 43

Henry has 1 dime and 2 nickels. How much money does he have?

A. 5 cents
B. 12 cents
C. 20 cents

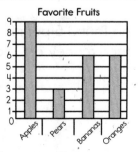
Favorite Fruits

Which 2 fruits were equally popular?

_____

1. 4 – 3 =

2. 9 – 4 =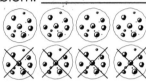

3. Write <, >, or = to make the statement true.

   57 ◯ 75

4. Ella had 8 cookies. Donna ate 4 cookies. How many cookies were left? Write a number sentence to show how you solved the problem. _____

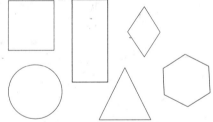

5. Which number sentence matches the picture?

   A. 5 – 3 = 2
   B. 4 + 2 = 6
   C. 4 – 2 = 2

6. Which numbers are between 16 and 19?

   A. 17 and 18
   B. 21 and 22
   C. 7 and 8

7. Draw base ten blocks to show 73.

8. Color the quadrilaterals.

9. Jan found 5 pennies on the sidewalk. How much money did she find? _____

10. What number does the flower represent? _____

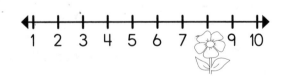

 2.OA.1, 2.OA.2, 2.NBT.1, 2.NBT.2, 2.NBT.4, 2.NBT.5, 2.MD.6, 2.MD.8, 2.G.1   CD-104591 • © Carson-Dellosa

Name_____

Day 1

Color the rectangles.

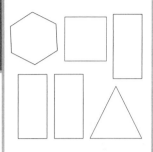

9 – 4 =

Day 2

Draw base ten blocks to show 20.

Mama Cat had 3 kittens. A family adopted 2 of the kittens. How many kittens did Mama Cat have left? Write a number sentence to show how you solved the problem.

_____

Look at the base ten blocks. Write the number shown.

_____

What time is shown? _____

Which number sentence matches the picture?

A. 7 + 3 = 10
B. 9 – 2 = 7
C. 8 + 4 = 12

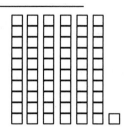

5 + 2 =

Day 3

11 – 4 =

What number does the cupcake represent? _____

18 19 20 🧁 22 23 24

Day 4

How long is the key? _____

What number is 10 more than 12?

_____

Is the number of flowers even or odd? _____

6 + 4 =

Logan had 2 dimes. He found 4 pennies in the couch cushions. How much money does Logan have now?

_____

Total Pies Baked

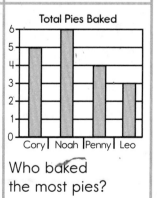

Who baked the most pies?

_____

Name_____

1. How many inches long is the watch?

   _____

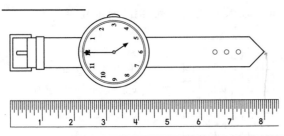

2. Draw base ten blocks to show 13.

3. What time is shown? _____

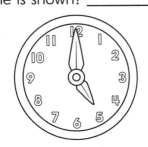

4. Who ate the least number of apples?

   _____

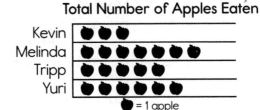

   Total Number of Apples Eaten

   Kevin
   Melinda
   Tripp
   Yuri

   = 1 apple

5. Is the number of frogs even or odd?

   _____

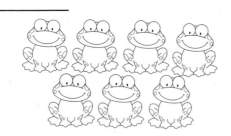

6. Kit had 8 marbles. She gave 5 to Leslie. How many did Kit have left? Write a number sentence to show how you solved the problem. _____

7. What number does the cupcake represent? _____

   13 14 15 16 17 🧁 19 20 21 22 23

8. 9 – 3 =

9. 9 – 6 =

10. 6 + 1 =

2.OA.1, 2.OA.2, 2.OA.3, 2.NBT.4, 2.MD.1, 2.MD.6, 2.MD.7, 2.MD.10   CD-104591 • © Carson-Dellosa

Name_____

Day 1

Write the number word for each number.

4 _____

10 _____

7 _____

Draw two different triangles.

Day 2

What time is shown?

_____

Count by 5s.

5, 10, 15,

_____,

_____,

_____

Tara had 4 lollipops and gave 1 of them away. How many lollipops did she have left? Write a number sentence to show how you solved the problem.

_____

---

11 – 6 = _____

9 – 6 = _____

8 – 2 = _____

Look at the base ten blocks. Write the number shown.

_____

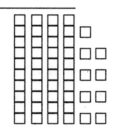

Write <, >, or = to make the statement true.

45 ◯ 54

Day 3

Write <, >, or = to make the statement true.

32 ◯ 30

If Amber has 1 nickel and Justin has 7 pennies, how much money do they have altogether?

_____

Day 4

Circle the longest line segment.

A. •———•
B. •————————•

Sam's fishing pole measured 5 feet. Blair's fishing pole measured 4 feet. How much longer is Sam's fishing pole than Blair's?

_____

---

5 + 5 =

Total Number of Books Read

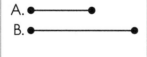

| | Gabe | Oliver | Quinn | Valerie |

Who read the least amount of books?

_____

---

5 + 2 = _____

3 + 1 = _____

8 + 0 = _____

Write the numbers that are between 24 and 29.

24, _____,

_____,

_____,

_____, 29

Name_____

1. What time is shown? _____

2. Draw a flat shape that has no straight sides or angles.

3. Count by 5s.

20, 25, 30, _____, _____,

_____

4. Eight cars were in the parking lot at the grocery store. Three drove away. How many cars are left in the parking lot? Write a number sentence to show how you solved the problem.

_____

5. What numbers come between 32 and 38? Count by 2s.

32, _____, _____, 38

6. Write the number word for each number.

14 _____

9 _____

1 _____

7. 8 − 3 =

8. 5 + 3 =

9. Write <, >, or = to make the statement true.

25 ◯ 35

10. Look at the base ten blocks. Write the number shown. _____

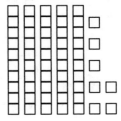

2.OA.1, 2.OA.2, 2.NBT.2, 2.NBT.3, 2.NBT.4, 2.MD.7, 2.G.1   CD-104591 • © Carson-Dellosa

Name_____

Day 1

Write the number that is 6 tens and 4 ones. _____

Draw two different rectangles.

There were 2 crayons, 5 markers, and 1 pencil in the drawer. How many writing tools were in the drawer? Write a number sentence to show how you solved the problem.

_____

6 + 4 = _____

9 – 2 = _____

4 + 1 = _____

Day 2

Look at the base ten blocks. Write the number shown.

_____

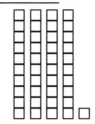

Count by 10s.

10, 20, 30,

_____,

_____,

_____

If Bonnie has 1 dime and 6 pennies, how much money does she have? _____

Write the number that is 10 more than 35.

_____

Day 3

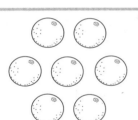

Is the number of oranges even or odd? _____

What time is shown? _____

Day 4

Total Scoops of Ice Cream Eaten

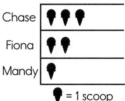

Chase
Fiona
Mandy

 = 1 scoop

How many scoops did all 3 children eat? _____

Write <, >, or = to make the statements true.

10 ◯ 12

33 ◯ 43

19 ◯ 19

Write the number word for each number.

4 _____

6 _____

8 _____

5 + 2 = _____

6 – 6 = _____

10 + 2 = _____

Add or subtract mentally.

52 + 10 = _____

44 – 10 = _____

20 + 10 = _____

4 – 2 =

Name_____

1. 6 + 3 =

2. 3 – 3 =

3. What number is 10 less than 68?

   _____

4. Brooke has 3 red beads and 2 blue beads. How many beads does she have? Write a number sentence to show how you solved the problem.

   _____

5. Dave has 4 pennies, Ivan has 6 pennies, and Grace has 3 pennies. How much money do the children have altogether?

   _____

6. Write <, >, or = to make the statements true.

   15 ◯ 11

   29 ◯ 12

   2 ◯ 16

7. What time is shown? _____

8. Write the number that is 3 tens and 6 ones. _____

9. Write the number word for each number.

   6 _____

   2 _____

   4 _____

10. Is the number of dogs even or odd?

    _____

    Write a number sentence to show a doubles fact. _____

    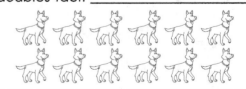

Name_____

Day 1

Write the number that shows 5 tens and 1 one.

_____

Circle the shapes that have 3 sides.

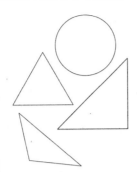

Day 2

Look at the base ten blocks. Write the number shown.

_____

Caden has 1 nickel and 1 penny. How much money does Caden have?

_____

Leo had 6 goldfish. He gave away 2 goldfish. How many goldfish does Leo have left? Write a number sentence to show how you solved the problem.

_____

5 – 4 = _____

8 + 3 = _____

8 - 3 = _____

What time is shown?

_____

What number does the star represent?

_____

Day 3

Write the number that is 10 less than each number shown.

_____ 38

_____ 45

_____ 22

How long is the adhesive bandage?

_____

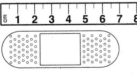

Pictures Taken by Mr. Ross

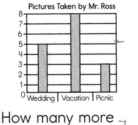

How many more vacation pictures were taken than picnic pictures?

_____

Day 4

Peter ate 4 grapes. Later, he ate 3 more grapes. How many grapes did Peter eat in all?

_____

Write the number for each number word.

twelve _____

nine _____

fourteen _____

6 – 4 = _____

8 + 2 = _____

4 + 6 = _____

Write <, >, or = to make the statement true.

15 ◯ 25

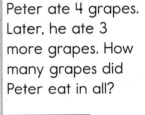

Is the number of birds even or odd?

_____

Name_____

1. 4 + 5 =	2. 8 – 4 =
3. Lamar had 3 dimes in his pocket. Norris gave him 1 nickel. How much money does Lamar have now? _____	4. The teacher has a cup with 5 pens in it. If 3 pens do not work, how many pens work? Write a number sentence to show how you solved the problem. _____
5. What time is shown? _____ 	6. Write the number that is 10 more than each number. 20 _____ 41 _____ 36 _____
7. Write the number that is 1 ten and 9 ones. _____	8. Circle the shape that is different.
9. Ginny has 5 dimes and 4 pennies. How much money does she have? _____	10. How many more students were absent from picture day in 2010 than in 2012? _____    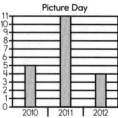

 2.OA.1, 2.OA.2, 2.NBT.1, 2.NBT.8, 2.MD.7, 2.MD.8, 2.MD.10, 2.G.1   CD-104591 • © Carson-Dellosa

Name_____

Day 1

Write the number that is 6 tens and 8 ones. _____

Circle the shapes that have 4 sides.

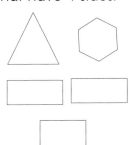

Perry spent 7 hours at the park on Saturday. On Sunday, she spent 8 hours at the park. How many hours did Perry spend at the park all weekend?

_____

14 – 10 = _____

14 + 10 = _____

Day 2

Jay decorated 15 chocolate cupcakes and 4 vanilla cupcakes. How many more chocolate cupcakes did Jay decorate?

_____

Look at the base ten blocks. Write the number shown. _____

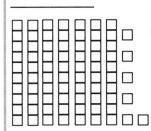

What time is shown?

_____

17 + 8 =

_____

16 + 11 =

_____

20 – 0 =

_____

Day 3

Count by 5s.

45, 50, 55,

_____ ,

_____ ,

_____

What number does the frog represent?

_____

27 28 29   31 32 33

Write <, >, or = to make the statements true.

52 ◯ 52

20 ◯ 30

45 ◯ 35

14 – 12 = _____

6 + 16 = _____

Day 4

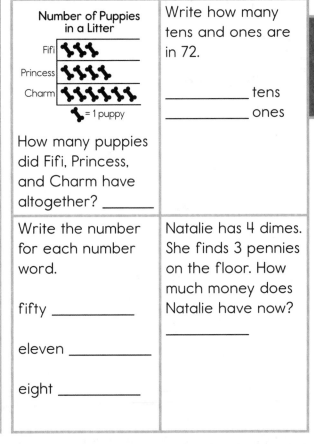

Number of Puppies in a Litter

Fifi

Princess

Charm

🦴 = 1 puppy

How many puppies did Fifi, Princess, and Charm have altogether? _____

Write how many tens and ones are in 72.

_____ tens

_____ ones

Write the number for each number word.

fifty _____

eleven _____

eight _____

Natalie has 4 dimes. She finds 3 pennies on the floor. How much money does Natalie have now?

_____

1. 16 + 6 =

2. 25 – 4 =

3. Count by 5s.

    30, 35, 40, _____, _____,
    _____

4. Tyler has 14 tennis balls. He loses 4 tennis balls. How many tennis balls does Tyler have now? Write a number sentence to show how you solved the problem.

    _____

5. What number does the chick represent?
    _____

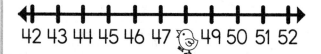

6.
Days with Temperatures
Above 100° Fahrenheit

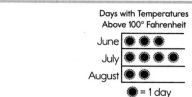

= 1 day

Look at the graph. How many days had temperatures above 100°F during June, July, and August? _____

7. Write the number for each number word.

    seventeen _____

    thirteen _____

    fifteen _____

8. How much money does Reba have if she has 5 nickels?

    A. 25 cents
    B. 20 cents
    C. 35 cents

9. What time is shown? _____

10. Write how many tens and ones are in 87.

    _____ tens
    _____ ones

 2.OA.1, 2.NBT.1, 2.NBT.2, 2.NBT.3, 2.NBT.5, 2.MD.6, 2.MD.7, 2.MD.8, 2.MD.10   CD-104591 • © Carson-Dellosa

Name_____

Day 1

Write the numbers.

8 tens, 9 ones

_____

7 tens, 3 ones

_____

4 tens, 8 ones

_____

What is the name of a shape that has 6 sides?

_____

Miguel has 18 pairs of shorts in his closet. He also has 12 shirts in his closet. How many items of clothing does Miguel have in his closet in all?

_____

$6 + 6 =$ _____

$5 + 9 =$ _____

$6 + 4 =$ _____

Day 2

Look at the base ten blocks. Write the number shown.

_____

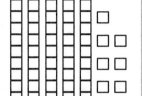

Is the number of leaves even or odd? _____

What time is shown?

_____

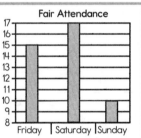

Count by 10s.

30, 40, 50,

_____,

_____,

_____

Day 3

Write <, >, or = to make the statements true.

45 ◯ 50

23 ◯ 21

80 ◯ 78

Wendy has 4 dimes and 2 pennies. How much money does Wendy have?

_____

What number does the bird represent?

_____

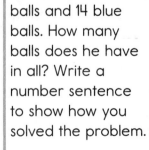

94 95 96 97 98 99 100

$15 + 15 =$ _____

$12 - 10 =$ _____

Day 4

Fair Attendance

How many people attended the fair on Saturday and Sunday? _____

Julio has 16 red balls and 14 blue balls. How many balls does he have in all? Write a number sentence to show how you solved the problem.

_____

$13 + 8 =$ _____

$14 + 9 =$ _____

$16 - 5 =$ _____

Look at the base ten blocks. Write the number shown.

_____

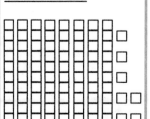

1. 17 − 11 =	2. 15 + 7 =

3. Wayne is seventh in line waiting for a store to open. There are 17 people waiting in line. How many people are in line behind Wayne?

_____

4. Write <, >, or = to make the statements true.

56 ◯ 49

83 ◯ 18

37 ◯ 25

5. Write the numbers.

4 tens, 1 one _____

2 tens, 9 ones _____

1 ten, 5 ones _____

6. Count by 10s.

50, 60, 70, _____, _____,

_____

7. What time is shown? _____

8. Is the number of eggs even or odd?

_____

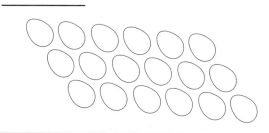

9. Maggie has 8 dimes. How much money does she have? _____

10. What number does the tree represent?

_____

83 84 85 86 87 🌲 89 90 91 92 93

Name_____

Day 1

Write the number 83 in expanded form.

_____

How many sides does this shape have? _____

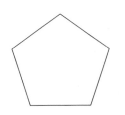

Day 2

Look at the base ten blocks. Write the number shown.

_____

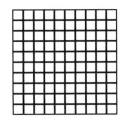

Write a number sentence for the picture. Then, solve the number sentence.

_____

Mario picks 28 flowers. Nora picks 16 flowers. How many more flowers does Mario pick than Nora? Write a number sentence to show how you solved the problem.

_____

17 – 6 = _____

17 + 3 = _____

Denise has 2 nickels and 2 pennies. How much money does Denise have?

_____

Count by 5s.

55, 60, 65,

_____,

_____,

Day 3

Write <, >, or = to make the statements true.

110 ◯ 78

53 ◯ 63

105 ◯ 101

Is the number of goldfish even or odd? _____

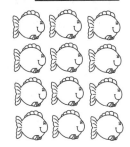

Day 4

What time is shown?

_____

Write the number for each number word.

twenty-six _____

fifty-three _____

thirty-two _____

What number does the crayon represent?

_____

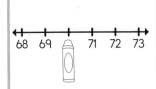
68 69   71 72 73

12 + 7 = _____

18 – 6 = _____

A total of 17 goldfish are being given away as prizes at the school carnival. If 6 of the goldfish are orange and the rest are yellow, how many of the goldfish are yellow?

_____

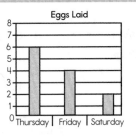

How many more eggs were laid on Thursday than on Friday? _____

1. 15 + 5 =

2. 23 − 4 =

3. Count by 5s.

   45, 50, 55, _____, _____,

   _____

4. What number does the goldfish represent? _____

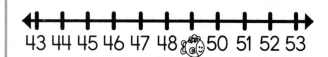

43 44 45 46 47 48 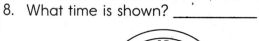 50 51 52 53

5. Dante's dog has 18 bones. His dog buries 4 bones. How many bones does his dog have now? Write a number sentence to show how you solved the problem.

   _____

6.

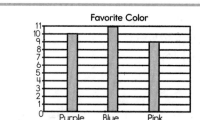

Favorite Color

Purple   Blue   Pink

   Look at the bar graph. Which color was the most popular? _____

7. Write the number for each number word.

   fifteen _____

   seventeen _____

   twenty-six _____

8. What time is shown? _____

9. Write <, >, or = to make the statements true.

   14 ◯ 12

   76 ◯ 112

10. Is the number of scissors even or odd?

    _____

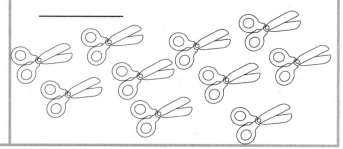

Name_____

Day 1

Write the number 98 in expanded form.

_____

How many sides does this shape have? _____

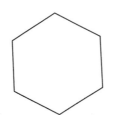

Timothy spends 18 days at the beach. It rains 16 of the days that Timothy is visiting the beach. How many days does it not rain?

_____

18 + 10 = _____

10 + 10 = _____

17 – 10 = _____

Day 2

Write how many hundreds, tens, and ones are in 105.

_____ hundred

_____ tens

_____ ones

Is the number of buttons even or odd? _____

Colby has 2 quarters in his pocket. Nikki gives Colby 5 pennies that she found on the floor. How much money does Colby have now?

_____

Count by 100s.

100, 200, 300,

_____ ,

_____ ,

_____

Day 3

Write the number word for each number.

13 _____

24 _____

43 _____

45 + 30 =

Write the number 15 on the number line.

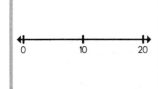

What time is shown? _____

Day 4

Favorite Snacks

Chips	🐞🐞🐞🐞
Pretzels	🐞🐞🐞🐞🐞🐞🐞🐞🐞🐞
Fruit	🐞🐞🐞🐞🐞🐞🐞🐞

🐞 = 2 votes

How many students voted for pretzels or fruit as their favorite snack?

_____

Jared had 20 cents. He bought a piece of candy for 15 cents. How much money does Jared have left? _____

Write <, >, or = to make the statements true.

125 ◯ 116

54 ◯ 23

98 ◯ 98

5 + _____ = 12

6 + _____ = 15

3 + _____ = 9

1. There are 12 campers in the lake for an afternoon swim. If 6 more campers join them, how many campers are in the lake in all? Write a number sentence to show how you solved the problem. _____

2. Write the numbers in expanded form.

   54 _____

   78 _____

3. Write how many hundreds, tens, and ones are in 121.

   _____ hundred
   _____ tens
   _____ one

4. What time is shown? _____

5. Chelsea has 2 quarters. How much money does she have? _____

6. Write the number word for each number.

   17 _____

   21 _____

   61 _____

7. 15 + 10 = _____

   24 + 10 = _____

   64 – 10 = _____

8. Count by 100s.

   300, 400, 500, _____, _____, _____

9. 37 + 22 =

10. Is the number of buttons even or odd? _____

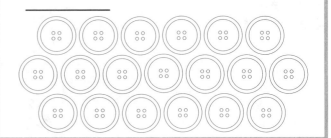

 2.OA.1, 2.OA.3, 2.NBT.1, 2.NBT.2, 2.NBT.3, 2.NBT.5, 2.NBT.8, 2.MD.7, 2.MD.8   CD-104591 • © Carson-Dellosa

Name_____

Day 1

Write each number.

4 hundreds, 3 tens, 2 ones

_____

2 hundreds, 4 ones

_____

Name this shape.

_____

Count by 5s.

105, 110, 115,

_____,

_____,

_____

Day 2

Molly has 1 dollar and 3 pennies. Philip has 1 dollar and 1 nickel. Who has more money?

_____

Joey is running a race that is 15 miles long. He stops to eat an energy bar after running 11 miles. How many miles does Joey have left to run?

_____

---

37 + 30 = _____

47 + 31 = _____

What time is shown?

_____

Look at the base ten blocks. Write the number shown.

_____

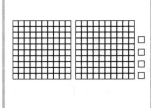

Day 3

Write the number that is 100 less than each number.

_____ 160

_____ 436

_____ 254

Is this number of carrots even or odd? _____

---

11 – 1 = _____

6 + 8 = _____

7 + 4 = _____

Day 4

Write the number sentence that the picture shows.

_____

Write <, >, or = to make the statements true.

154 ◯ 145

179 ◯ 199

203 ◯ 230

Kayla rakes 14 piles of leaves in her front yard and 15 piles of leaves in her backyard. How many piles of leaves does Kayla rake in all?

_____

Write the number for each number word.

sixteen _____

twenty-one _____

nineteen _____

Neil has 1 dollar and 1 dime. Mandy gives him 5 pennies. How much money does Neil have now?

A. $1.25
B. $1.15
C. $1.05

---

1. Look at the base ten blocks. Write the number shown. _____

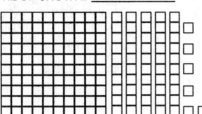

2. 26 + 53 =

3. Mrs. Lopez makes 20 cupcakes for her daughter's class. She puts sprinkles on 10 of the cupcakes. How many of the cupcakes does Mrs. Lopez not put sprinkles on?

_____

4. If you have 1 dollar and 1 quarter, how much money do you have?

   A. $1.45
   B. $1.75
   C. $1.25

5. Write the number.

   5 hundreds, 3 tens, 2 ones

   _____

6. Count by 5s.

   225, 230, 235, _____, _____,

   _____

7. Write the number that is 100 more than each number.

   326 _____

   455 _____

   200 _____

8. 3 + 4 = _____

   12 – 4 = _____

   6 + 3 = _____

9. What time is shown? _____

10. Is the number of keys even or odd?

   _____

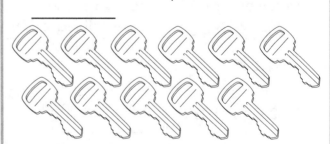

Name_____

Day 1

Write <, >, or = to make the statement true.

43 $\bigcirc$ 14

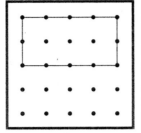

How many square units make up the rectangle? _____

William attended swim class for 15 hours in June and 15 hours in July. How many total hours did William attend swimming lessons?

_____

3 + 5 = _____

9 + 6 = _____

8 + 2 = _____

Day 2

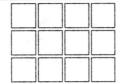

Which equation matches the array?

A. 4 + 4 + 4 = 12
B. 3 + 3 = 6
C. 5 + 5 + 5 + 5 = 20

Count by 10s.

340, 350, 360,

_____ ,

_____ ,

_____

What time is shown?

_____

82 – 31 = _____

26 + 53 = _____

Day 3

Draw two ways to make $1.00.

Look at the base 10 blocks. Write the number shown.

_____

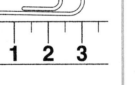

Write the expanded form of 389.

_____

Write the number that is 10 less than each number shown.

_____ 450

_____ 290

_____ 110

Day 4

How long is the paper clip?

_____

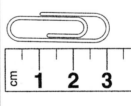

Is the number of keys even or odd?

_____

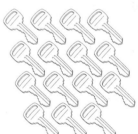

Write the number word for each number.

31 _____

55 _____

72 _____

4 + 2 = _____

8 + 7 = _____

3 + 6 = _____

1. Rashad has 17 CDs in his music collection. James has 14 more CDs than Rashad. How many CDs does James have? _____

2. $52 + 42 =$

3. What time is shown? _____

4. Draw one way to make 64 cents.

5.

Which equation matches the array?

A. $2 + 2 + 2 + 2 + 2 = 10$
B. $3 + 3 + 3 + 3 + 3 + 3 = 18$
C. $2 + 2 + 2 = 6$

6. Count by 10s.

540, _____, 560, 570, _____,

_____

7. $8 + 4 =$ _____

$7 + 3 =$ _____

$1 + 8 =$ _____

8. $88 - 53 =$

9.

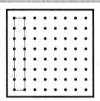

How many square units make up the rectangle? _____

10. Mr. and Ms. Rizzo have 9 grandchildren. If 7 of their grandchildren have red hair and the rest of their grandchildren have brown hair, how many of their grandchildren have brown hair?

_____

2.OA.1, 2.OA.2, 2.OA.4, 2.NBT.2, 2.NBT.5, 2.MD.7, 2.MD.8, 2.G.2 CD-104591 • © Carson-Dellosa

Name_____

Day 1

Ana buys 10 bubble wands to give away as birthday presents. She gives away 7 bubble wands during the school year. How many bubble wands does Ana have left?

_____

Count by 100s.

320, 420,

_____,

_____,

_____

Look at the base ten blocks. Write the number shown.

_____

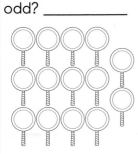

$5 + 5 =$ _____

$4 + 8 =$ _____

$6 + 9 =$ _____

Day 2

Write the number for each number word.

forty-five

_____

eighty-eight

_____

ninety-three

_____

Write <, >, or = to make the statements true.

145 ◯ 165

78 ◯ 87

What time is shown?

_____

Which equation matches the array?

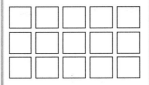

A. $8 + 8 = 16$
B. $5 + 5 + 5 = 15$
C. $8 + 8 + 8 = 24$

Day 3

Jimmy has 55 cents in his pocket. Draw the coins that Jimmy could have in his pocket.

$86 - 51 =$

Is the number of lollipops even or odd? _____

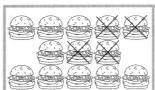

Shannon writes the numbers 17 and 16. She asks her brother to add the numbers and write the total. If he is correct, what number should Shannon's brother write? _____

Day 4

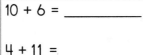

Write the number sentence that the picture shows. Then, solve the number sentence.

_____

Draw base ten blocks to show 651.

$10 + 6 =$ _____

$4 + 11 =$

_____

$12 + 2 =$ _____

$14 + 34 =$

Name_____

1. 7 + 6 = _____

   5 + 2 = _____

   9 + 6 = _____

2. Which equation matches the array?

   A. 6 + 6 + 6 = 18
   B. 4 + 4 + 4 + 4 = 16
   C. 2 + 2 + 2 + 2 = 8

3. Tiffany is putting together a wagon. The instruction book is 13 pages long. She has read the first 8 pages of the book. How many pages does Tiffany have left to read? _____

4. 67 − 42 =

5. Count by 100s.

   510, 610, _____, _____,

   _____

6. Write <, >, or = to make the statements true.

   168 ◯ 145

   264 ◯ 364

7. Brianna has 82 cents in her purse. Draw the coins that Brianna could have in her purse.

8. Draw base ten blocks to show 376.

9. What time is shown? _____

10. 13 + 43 =

 2.OA.1, 2.OA.2, 2.OA.4, 2.NBT.1, 2.NBT.2, 2.NBT.4, 2.NBT.5, 2.MD.7, 2.MD.8 CD-104591 • © Carson-Dellosa

Name_____

Day 1

2 + 8 = _____

3 + 7 = _____

4 + 5 = _____

What is the value of the number 3 in the number 356?

_____

Michelle has 3 quarters and 6 nickels. How much money does Michelle have?

_____

Count by 5s.

355, 360, 365,

_____,

_____,

_____

Day 2

Write the number that is 100 more than each number.

491 _____

342 _____

847 _____

Lola makes cookies for 16 of her neighbors. She puts chocolate chip cookies in 13 baskets. She puts oatmeal cookies in the rest of the baskets. How many baskets have oatmeal cookies?

_____

Write the number sentence that the picture shows.

_____

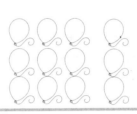

---

75 – 25 =

Day 3

What time is shown?

_____

Write an addition equation for the array.

□ □ □ □
□ □ □ □

_____

Draw base ten blocks to show 169.

There are 13 monkeys at the zoo. If 9 of the monkeys are swinging from trees, how many monkeys are not swinging from trees? _____

Day 4

Write the number word for each number.

30 _____

61 _____

73 _____

Circle the dog that has an odd number of spots.

---

94 – 60 =

Write <, >, or = to make the statements true.

37 ◯ 33

123 ◯ 132

46 ◯ 46

1. What time is shown? _____

2. 32 + 51 = 83

3. Jeremy buys a box of 20 paper clips. He uses 15 paper clips during the school year. How many paper clips does Jeremy have left? _____

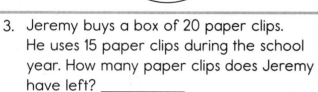

4. 9 – 8 = _____

   8 – 2 = _____

   6 – 4 = _____

5. Nellie has 8 dimes. Lynn gives her 2 nickels. How much money does Nellie have now? _____

6. Write <, >, or = to make the statements true.

   17 < 77

   38 > 21

   102 < 201

7. Write an addition equation for the array.

   _____

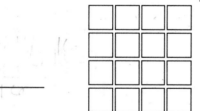

8. 98 – 77 =

9. Draw base ten blocks to show 305.

10. Circle the tree that has an even number of apples on it.

 2.OA.1, 2.OA.2, 2.OA.4, 2.NBT.3, 2.NBT.4, 2.NBT.5, 2.MD.7, 2.MD.8   CD-104591 • © Carson-Dellosa

Name_____

Day 1

Draw the hands on the clock to show 12:30.

Write <, >, or = to make the statements true.

203 ◯ 233

400 ◯ 300

555 ◯ 556

Byron has 4 dimes and 5 pennies. Draw another way to show the amount of money that Byron has.

Day 2

Look at the base ten blocks. Write the number shown.

_____

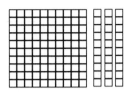

Write the number that is 10 more than each number.

110 _____

620 _____

880 _____

7 + 5 = _____

5 + 9 = _____

9 + 7 = _____

Circle the box that has an odd number of tallies.

26 + 41 =

Day 3

Madeline bought 16 picture frames. Later, she saw a sale on picture frames and bought 14 more picture frames. How many picture frames did Madeline buy in all?

_____

Write the numbers.

3 hundreds, 5 ones

_____

9 hundreds, 2 tens, 3 ones

_____

Write an addition equation for the array.

_____

Day 4

Laura has a vase with 21 roses in it. Nine are red roses, and the rest are white. How many of the roses are white? _____

Count by 10s.

340, 350,

_____,

_____,

380, 390

12 + 10 + 13 =

Jasper has 1 quarter, 1 dime, and 5 pennies. How much money does Jasper have?

_____

36 + 31 =

© Carson-Dellosa • CD-104591

39

1. 1 + 5 = _____

   5 + 3 = _____

   3 + 4 = _____

2. 65 + 34 =

3. 15 + 17 + 10 =

4. Marcus has 18 beads. If 12 of the beads are orange and the rest of the beads are red, how many red beads does Marcus have? _____

5. Wyatt has 6 nickels and 10 pennies. Draw another way to show the amount of money that Wyatt has.

6. Draw the hands on the clock to show 3:00.

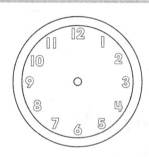

7. Write an addition equation for the array.

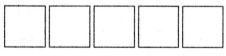

   _____

8. Write <, >, or = to make the statements true.

   216 261

   44 ◯ 34

9. Count by 10s.

   810, _____, _____, 840, 850

10. Write the numbers.

    7 hundreds, 4 tens, 7 ones _____

    2 hundreds, 7 ones _____

Day 1

Write the expanded form of each number.

230 _____

573 _____

Draw two ways to show 50 cents.

Day 2

Draw the hands on the clock to show 5:30.

Count by 100s.

345, 445,

_____, 645,

_____

Write the number that is 100 less than each number.

_____ 655

_____ 248

_____ 213

A large department store sold 25 alarm clocks. By the end of the week, 9 alarm clocks had been returned. How many alarm clocks were not returned?

_____

What is the value of the 8 in each number?

817 _____

228 _____

180 _____

Write the number word for each number.

18 _____

64 _____

5 _____

Day 3

16 + 19 + 20 =

4 – 3 = _____

9 – 6 = _____

8 – 4 = _____

Tasha has 16 sweaters. If 9 of the sweaters are wool, how many of the sweaters are not wool?

_____

Day 4

64 – 31 =

72 + 12 =

Write <, >, or = to make the statements true.

901 ◯ 910

431 ◯ 413

240 ◯ 204

3 + 7 = _____

6 + 6 = _____

10 + 1 = _____

Draw base ten blocks to show 199.

Name_____

1. Draw two ways to show 75 cents.	2. 22 + 33 + 10 =
3. 37 − 22 =	4. 44 + 25 =
5. Cynthia has 19 bananas. Ashton has 13 bananas. How many bananas do Cynthia and Ashton have altogether? _____	6. Draw the hands on the clock to show 7:00. 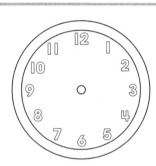
7. 10 + 6 = _____ 7 − 5 = _____	8. What is the value of the 3 in each number? 435 _____ 35 _____ 203 _____
9. Write <, >, or = to make the statements true. 204 ◯ 240 167 ◯ 176 203 ◯ 23	10. Write the expanded form of each number. 107 _____ 320 _____

 2.OA.1, 2.OA.2, 2.NBT.1, 2.NBT.3, 2.NBT.4, 2.NBT.5, 2.NBT.6, 2.MD.7, 2.MD.8   CD-104591 • © Carson-Dellosa

Name_____

Day 1

Jarvis has 1 dime and 3 nickels. Draw another way to show how much money Jarvis has.

24 + 10 + 32 =

Draw base ten blocks to show 320.

48 – 24 =

Day 2

The tennis club starts its season with 25 tennis balls. During the first week of practice, 16 balls were lost. How many tennis balls are left?
_____

Look at the base ten blocks. Write the number shown.
_____

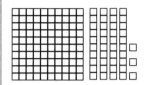

Add mentally.

545 + 100 =
_____

350 + 10 =
_____

Count by 100s.

515, 615, 715,

_____,

_____

Day 3

Write an addition equation for the array.

_____

Circle the T-shirt that has an even number of black stripes on it.

Day 4

Draw the hands on the clock to show 11:30.

Write <, >, or = to make the statements true.

47 ◯ 37

105 ◯ 115

57 ◯ 75

A chef cracked 19 eggs. A few minutes later, he cracked an additional 3 eggs. How many eggs did the chef crack in all? _____

55 + 22 =

Patrick has 2 quarters and 7 pennies. How much money does Patrick have?
_____

7 + 5 = _____

4 + 4 = _____

9 + 6 = _____

1. 55 + 11 =

2. 56 – 22 =

3. 5 – 4 = _____

    7 – 2 = _____

4. Write an addition equation for the array.

    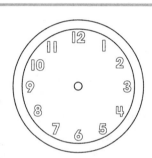

    _____

5. Draw the hands on the clock to show 9:00.

6. Daysha has 8 dimes. She finds 5 pennies on the sidewalk. How much money does Daysha have altogether? _____

7. Sasha has 18 magazines about doll collecting and 17 magazines about outdoor games. How many magazines about doll collecting and outdoor games does Sasha have? _____

8. 50 + 10 + 12 =

9. Count by 100s.

    120, 220, _____, _____,

    _____

10. Draw base ten blocks to show 193.

Name_____

Day 1

28 – 15 =	20 + 10 + 56 =

| Circle the ice-cream cone that has an even number of sprinkles.  | Look at the base ten blocks. Write the number shown. _____ 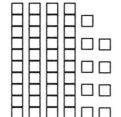 |

Day 2

5 – 5 = _____ 7 – 4 = _____ 9 – 1 = _____	Jamal checked out 15 books from the library in June. He checked out 20 books in July. How many more books did Jamal check out in July than in June? _____

| Draw base ten blocks to show 215. | Write the number sentence that the picture shows. _____  |

Day 3

Mr. Pappas has 27 students in his class. If 13 of the students are boys and the rest are girls, how many girls are there in Mr. Pappas' class? _____	Count by 5s. 605, 610, _____, _____, _____

| 8 + 7 = _____

7 + 2 = _____

9 + 0 = _____ | Blain earned 3 nickels on Thursday and 9 dimes on Tuesday. How much money does he have? _____ |

Day 4

62 + 34 =	Write <, >, or = to make the statements true. 230 ◯ 203 37 ◯ 370 405 ◯ 405

| Draw an array for the equation.
2 + 2 + 2 = 6 | What time is shown? _____  |

Name_____

1. Draw an array for the equation.
   4 + 4 + 4 + 4 + 4 = 20

2. Brantley earned 6 nickels on Saturday and 5 nickels on Sunday. How much money did Brantley earn over the weekend? _____

3. 10 + 3 = _____

   5 + 4 = _____

   7 + 2 = _____

4. 64 + 25 =

5. 75 – 42 =

6. What time is shown?
   _____

7. There are 36 books in Luke's bedroom. Eighteen of the books are nonfiction, and the rest of the books are fiction. How many of the books in Luke's bedroom are fiction? _____

8. 50 + 19 + 10 =

9. Write <, >, or = to make the statements true.

   99 ◯ 98

   112 ◯ 121

   444 ◯ 434

10. Count by 5s.

    125, 130, _____, _____,

    _____

46   2.OA.1, 2.OA.2, 2.OA.4, 2.NBT.2, 2.NBT.4, 2.NBT.5, 2.NBT.6, 2.MD.7, 2.MD.8   CD-104591 • © Carson-Dellosa

Name_____

Day 1

What time is shown?
_____

Count by 10s.

430, 440,

_____,

_____,

_____

Day 2

Zane has 9 dimes and 5 pennies. Draw another way to show how much money Zane has.

Look at the base ten blocks. Write the number shown.
_____

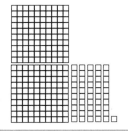

Circle the box that has an odd number of tallies.

7 + 7 = _____

6 + 5 = _____

3 + 9 = _____

Draw an array for the equation.
5 + 5 + 5 = 15

6 – 1 = _____

9 – 5 = _____

8 – 8 = _____

Day 3

88 – 66 =

Write the number word for each number.

300 _____

152 _____

75 + 24 =

Day 4

Write the expanded form of 405.

_____

Add mentally.

304 + 100 = _____

15 + 10 = _____

55 + 5 = _____

Crystal and Davis each juggle 11 balls during recess. How many balls do Crystal and Davis juggle in all?

_____

Samantha sees 14 butterflies and 12 spiders on a nature walk. How many more butterflies than spiders does Samantha see on her walk?

_____

72 + 14 + 10 =

1. Draw an array for the equation.
   3 + 3 + 3 + 3 + 3 = 15

2. Travis earned 2 quarters and 4 dimes. Draw another way to show how much money Travis earned.

3. What time is shown? _____

4. 10 + 5 = _____

   8 + 5 = _____

   1 + 7 = _____

5. 23 + 14 =

6. 56 + 22 + 11 =

7. Circle the flower that has an odd number of petals.

8. Which is the expanded form of 345?

   A. 300 + 40 + 5
   B. 300 + 45
   C. 300 + 5

9. A total of 16 students order vegetable sandwiches for lunch. A total of 24 students order turkey sandwiches for lunch. How many students order sandwiches for lunch? _____

10. 97 − 33 =

 2.OA.1, 2.OA.2, 2.OA.3, 2.OA.4, 2.NBT.3, 2.NBT.5, 2.NBT.6, 2.MD.7, 2.MD.8   CD-104591 • © Carson-Dellosa

Name_____

Day 1

8 – 5 = _____

9 – 7 = _____

11 + 6 = _____

99 – 65 = _____

78 – 41 = _____

Write <, >, or = to make the statements true.

451 ◯ 541

329 ◯ 309

25 ◯ 205

34 + 12 + 40 =

Day 2

What time is shown?

_____

16 + 60 = _____

75 + 24 = _____

Circle the box that has an odd number of tallies.

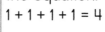

Count by 10s.

720, 730,

_____ ,

_____ ,

_____

Day 3

Ava has 67 cents in her coin purse. Draw one way to show 67 cents.

Liza sharpens 11 pencils Monday and 19 pencils Tuesday. How many more pencils does Liza sharpen on Tuesday?

_____

40 + 22 + 15 =

Write the number word for each number.

210 _____

603 _____

Day 4

Draw an array for the equation.
1 + 1 + 1 + 1 = 4

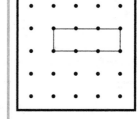

How many square units make up the rectangle?

_____

Before lunch, there are 28 cookies in Grandma's cookie jar. After lunch, there are only 19 cookies in Grandma's cookie jar. How many cookies were eaten at lunch?

_____

Draw base ten blocks to show 257.

Name_____

1.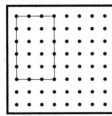

   How many square units make up the rectangle? _____

2. 4 + 9 = _____

   8 + 8 = _____

   7 – 4 = _____

3. What time is shown? _____

4. Draw an array for the equation.
   2 + 2 + 2 + 2 = 8

5. 37 + 51 = _____

   61 + 30 = _____

6. Tyler has 28 baseball cards. He gives away 12 of his cards. How many cards does Tyler have left? _____

7. Mr. Hoffman gave Brandon 95 cents for helping him around the house. Draw one way to show the money that Brandon has.

8. Count by 10s.

   810, _____, _____, 840, 850

9. 31 + 16 + 22 =

10. Write the number word for each number.

    415 _____

    112 _____

Name_____

Day 1

Jacob writes 27 letters while he is away at camp. He has 19 stamps. How many more stamps does Jacob need to mail all of his letters?

_____

Monique has $3.54. Draw 2 ways to show the amount of money Monique has.

Write the number for each number word.

three hundred fifty-six

_____

seven hundred twenty-one

_____

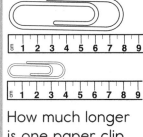

How much longer is one paper clip than the other?

_____

Day 2

2 + 12 = _____

9 + 3 = _____

1 + 4 = _____

39 + 97 = _____

40 – 19 = _____

51 + 22 + 10 + 13 =

Ryan has 48 feet of ribbon and Sierra has 21 feet of ribbon. How many feet of ribbon do they have altogether?

_____

Day 3

486 + 313 =

Write <, >, or = to make the statements true.

847 ◯ 784

116 ◯ 161

324 ◯ 234

887 – 354 =

Write the number 40 on the number line.

◄————————►
0   50

Day 4

Which units would you use to measure your pencil?

A. centimeters
B. meters

Count by 100s.

270, 370,

_____,

_____,

_____

Travon checked out 27 library books last year. Paul checked out 34 library books last year. How many library books did Travon and Paul check out altogether?

_____

What time is shown?

_____

Name_____

---

1. What time is shown? _____

2. Write the number 60 on the number line.

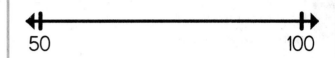

50   100

---

3. Connor has 11 centimeters of green string and 19 centimeters of purple string to put on his birthday balloons. How much total string does Connor have for the balloons? _____

4.

How much longer is one adhesive bandage than the other? _____

---

5. $639 + 250 =$

6. $427 - 211 =$

---

7. $65 + 47 =$ _____

$75 - 23 =$ _____

8. $7 + 3 =$ _____

$5 + 5 =$ _____

$6 + 3 =$ _____

---

9. Ms. Oritz grades 33 papers on Monday and 19 papers on Tuesday. How many more papers did Ms. Oritz grade on Monday than on Tuesday? _____

10. Write <, >, or = to make the statements true.

80 ◯ 50

260 ◯ 206

546 ◯ 654

 2.OA.1, 2.OA.2, 2.NBT.4, 2.NBT.5, 2.NBT.7, 2.MD.4, 2.MD.5, 2.MD.6, 2.MD.7   CD-104591 • © Carson-Dellosa

Name_____

Day 1

Write the number 60 on the number line.

20 ———————————— 70

10 – 8 = _____

12 – 7 = _____

5 – 2 = _____

57 + 10 + 6 =

674 – 124 =

Day 2

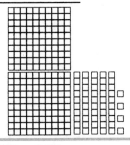

How tall is the ice-cream cone?

_____

Look at the base ten blocks. Write the number shown.

_____

Tristan has $2.71 in his pocket. Draw one way to show the money that Tristan has in his pocket.

412 – 387 =

Day 3

Miranda has 11 inches of border for the bulletin board. She needs 27 inches. How much more border does Miranda need to finish the bulletin board?

_____

Circle the box that has an odd number of tallies.

Draw an array for the equation.
5 + 5 + 5 = 15

Edgar washes 26 shirts. He needs to fold 18 shirts. How many shirts does Edgar not need to fold?

_____

Day 4

Write an addition equation for the array. _____

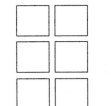

62 – 48 =

_____

44 + 25 =

_____

Count by 10s.

210, 220,

_____,

240, _____,

_____

Draw the hands on the clock to show 9:15.

1. 675 – 243 =	2. 563 – 416 =

3. 6 – 4 = _____ 12 – 3 = _____ 9 – 9 = _____	4. Write the number 20 on the number line. 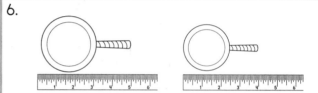 10 60

5. Mrs. Shaw bought 27 yards of fabric to make curtains for her classroom. Ms. Wolf bought 36 yards of fabric to make curtains for her classroom. How much fabric did Mrs. Shaw and Ms. Wolf buy in all? _____	6.  How many inches longer is one lollipop than the other? _____

7. Draw the hands on the clock to show 10:50.	8. There are 15 baseball games during the season. If 3 of the games are rained out, how many games are played? _____

9. Becky has $4.50 in her change purse. Draw one way to show how much money Becky has in her change purse.	10. How many inches longer is one pen than the other? _____ 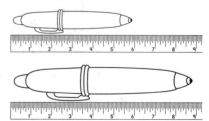

Name_____

Day 1

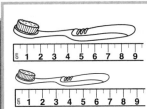

How much longer is one toothbrush than the other?

_____

Write the number 40 on the number line.

10   80

Write the number for each number word.

five hundred seventeen

_____

one hundred thirty-six

_____

697 – 463 =

Day 2

What time is shown?

_____

79 – 73 =

_____

84 + 14 =

_____

Which unit would you use to tell how long a school bus is?

A. centimeters
B. inches
C. meters

Ben pulled 2 one-dollar bills, 1 quarter, 1 dime, 4 nickels, and 10 pennies from his piggy bank. How much money does Ben have?

_____

Day 3

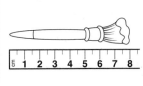

How long is the paintbrush?

_____

Leigh caught 14 fish one morning. Later the same day, she caught 14 more fish. How many fish did Leigh catch in all? _____

14 + 23 + 41 + 19 =

11 + 9 = _____

12 + 7 = _____

10 + 10 = _____

Day 4

574 + 225 =

Write an equation for the array.

_____

Write <, >, or = to make the statements true.

300 ◯ 30

462 ◯ 462

54 ◯ 541

A fisherman had 20 feet of fishing line. His line got stuck, and he had to cut away 13 feet. How many feet of fishing line does the fisherman have left? _____

1. 68 + 75 = _____

    66 − 29 = _____

2. 11 + 4 = _____

    12 + 10 = _____

    4 + 2 = _____

3. What time is shown? _____

4. Casey's mother put 4 one-dollar bills, 2 quarters, 4 dimes, 1 nickel, and 5 pennies in an envelope for Casey to use at the book fair. How much money did Casey's mother give Casey for the book fair?

    _____

5. 715 − 704 =

6.

    cm 1 2 3 4 5 6 7 8

    How long is the crayon? _____

7.

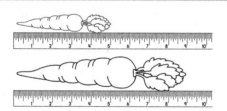

    How many inches longer is one carrot than the other? _____

8. Vanessa's yo-yo string measures 32 inches. Tony's yo-yo string measures 47 inches. How many inches of yo-yo string do Vanessa and Tony have altogether? _____

9. Emma ran 32 minutes on Saturday and 43 minutes on Sunday. How many more minutes did Emma run on Sunday?

    _____

10. 52 + 12 + 17 + 41 =

2.OA.1, 2.OA.2, 2.NBT.5, 2.NBT.6, 2.NBT.7, 2.MD.1, 2.MD.4, 2.MD.5, 2.MD.7, 2.MD.8   CD-104591 • © Carson-Dellosa

Day 1

There are 33 students in Jenna's class picture. If 25 of the students are smiling, how many students are not smiling?

_____

Write <, >, or = to make the statements true.

338 ◯ 318

56 ◯ 506

440 ◯ 404

Day 2

What time is shown?

_____

Is the number of shaded circles even or odd? _____

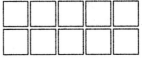

Anton is 60 inches tall. Abigail is 51 inches tall. How many inches taller is Anton than Abigail?

_____

958 – 947 =

How much longer is one leaf than the other? _____

9 + 9 = _____

4 + 6 = _____

12 – 6 = _____

Day 3

200 + 300 =

Write the number word for each number.

354 _____

902 _____

Day 4

What number is 5 tens and 6 ones?

_____

Write an equation for the array.

_____

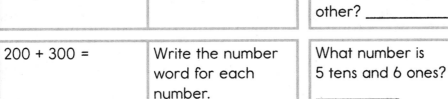

Jaelynn has 49 blocks in a bag. If 27 of the blocks are square and the rest are rectangular, how many of the blocks are rectangular?

_____

58 + 26 =

_____

90 – 11 =

_____

What unit would you use to measure a soccer field?

A. centimeters
B. inches
C. yards

Jordan was selling frozen ice treats. Blake gave Jordan 2 quarters and 2 nickels. How much did Blake pay for the treat?

_____

1.

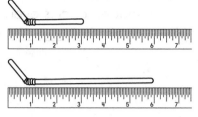

How many inches longer is one straw than the other? _____

2. Matthew's dad is 70 inches tall. Orlando's dad is 78 inches tall. How much taller is Orlando's dad than Matthew's?

_____

3. Melissa has 33 scarves in her closet. If 19 of the scarves are silk, how many of the scarves are not silk? _____

4. What unit would you use to measure a paper clip?

   A. centimeters
   B. feet
   C. meters

5. Kyle bought candy at the candy store. Kyle gave the candy store clerk 3 one-dollar bills, 2 dimes, 3 nickels, and 4 pennies. How much money did Kyle give the store clerk? _____

6. 11 – 5 = _____

   10 – 9 = _____

   6 + 1 = _____

7. What time is shown? _____

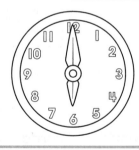

8. 400 – 300 =

9. Write the number that is 6 tens, 4 hundreds, and 5 ones.

   _____

10. Is the number of shaded triangles even or odd? _____

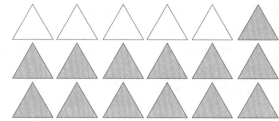

Name_____

Day 1

11 – 0 = _____

8 – 6 = _____

12 – 11 = _____

856 – 431 =

Write the number that is 6 ones, 3 hundreds, and 9 tens.

_____

Jason delivers groceries. On Saturday, he delivers 31 items. On Sunday, he delivers 48 items. How many items does Jason deliver on Saturday and Sunday combined?

_____

Day 2

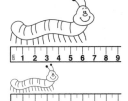

How much longer is one caterpillar than the other?

_____

Count by 100s.

550, 650,

_____,

_____,

_____

Subtract mentally.

430 – 100 =

_____

530 – 10 =

_____

634 + 14 =

Day 3

Write the number 25 on the number line.

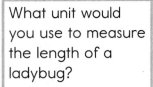
10   60

34 + 56 =

_____

78 – 35 =

_____

---

20 + 45 + 37 =

Megan has $4.00. She earns $2.50 more. How much money does Megan have now?

_____

Day 4

What unit would you use to measure the length of a ladybug?

A. meters
B. centimeters
C. feet

What time is shown?

_____

Write <, >, or = to make the statements true.

16 ◯ 14

249 ◯ 429

90 ◯ 109

Lindsey's necklace measured 17 inches. Dominique's necklace measured 25 inches. How much longer is Dominique's necklace than Lindsey's?

_____

1. Erica has $0.55. Later, she finds $0.25. How much money does Erica have now?

   _____

2. $362 + 332 =$

3. Nicole has 78 beads in a container. If 16 beads fall out, how many beads does Nicole have left? _____

4.

   How much longer is one umbrella than the other? _____

5. $7 - 2 =$ _____

   $9 - 5 =$ _____

   $7 + 12 =$ _____

6. What time is shown? _____

7. What unit would you use to measure the length of a door?

   A. centimeters
   B. inches
   C. feet

8. Alfonzo's belt is 55 inches long. Joshua's belt is 70 inches long. How much longer is Joshua's belt than Alfonzo's? _____

9. Write the number that is 7 tens, 8 ones, and 2 hundreds. _____

10. Add or subtract mentally.

    $390 + 100 =$ _____

    $78 - 10 =$ _____

Name_____

Day 1

Kennedy has $0.92. Her sister gives her $0.08. How much money does Kennedy have now? _____

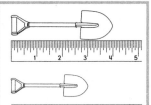

How many inches longer is one shovel than the other? _____

87 + 13 =

_____

91 – 35 =

_____

8 + 10 = _____

3 + 8 = _____

7 + 9 = _____

Day 2

Jonathan has 20 pieces of candy. He eats 6 pieces of candy. How many pieces of candy does he have left?

_____

Write the number 110 on the number line.

$\longleftrightarrow$
100   150

Write the standard form for each expanded form.

400 + 20 + 7

_____

900 + 9

_____

667 + 300 =

Day 3

Britney gets a haircut and has 5 inches cut off. Delaney gets a haircut and has 7 inches cut off. How much total hair did the girls have cut off?

_____

What unit would you use to measure the length of a dresser?

A. feet
B. inches
C. meters

Is the number of shaded squares even or odd?

_____

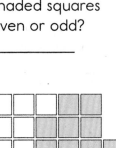

498 – 268 =

Day 4

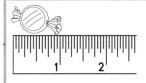

How many inches long is the piece of candy?

_____

Mason records 18 songs on Thursday and 17 songs on Friday. How many songs did Mason record altogether?

_____

12 + 13 + 56 + 48 =

Draw the hands on the clock to show 11:55.

1. 22 + 64 + 15 + 3 =

2. Scott has a total of $0.33. If he gives away $0.15, how much money will Scott have left? _____

3. 2 + 8 = _____

   6 + 7 = _____

   11 – 8 = _____

4.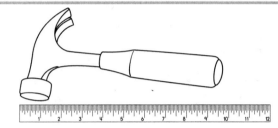

   How many inches long is the hammer?

   _____

5. Draw the hands on the clock to show 12:10.

   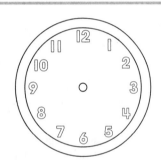

6. Anna and Clarissa grilled 44 hamburgers and 61 hot dogs at their cookout. How many hamburgers and hot dogs did they grill in all? _____

7. 450 + 246 =

8. 397 – 231 =

9.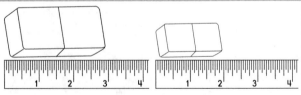

   How many inches longer is one eraser than the other? _____

10. Hannah's dog can jump 8 feet in the air. Maricela's dog can jump 6 feet in the air. How much higher can Hannah's dog jump than Maricela's? _____

Name_____

Day 1

What time is shown?

_____

What unit would you use to measure a marker?

A. feet
B. meters
C. inches

Write <, >, or = to make the statements true.

50 ◯ 150

918 ◯ 98

51 ◯ 51

333 – 222 =

Day 2

Dustin has $0.38 in his pocket. At lunch, he lends Jack $0.15. How much money does Dustin have now?

_____

Write the number 120 on the number line.

◀━━━━━━━━━━━━▶
100   200

Add or subtract mentally.

460 – 100 =

_____

540 + 10 =

_____

738 + 261 =

Day 3

Ethan spends 40 minutes mowing his front lawn and 15 minutes mowing his back lawn. How many more minutes does Ethan spend mowing his front lawn than his back lawn? _____

Write the number word for each number.

422 _____

72 _____

How tall is the water bottle?

_____

Day 4

56 – 27 =

_____

61 + 27 =

_____

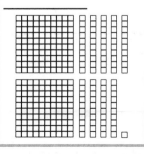

How much longer is one spoon than the other? _____

4 – 4 = _____

9 – 8 = _____

9 + 2 = _____

Look at the base ten blocks. Write the number shown.

_____

Brian is using a ladder that measures 96 inches. Derek is using a ladder that measures 60 inches. How much taller is Brian's ladder than Derek's?

_____

1. Cindy planted a maple tree in her yard that was 65 inches tall. Over the next year, the tree grew 23 inches. How tall is the maple tree now? _____

2. What time is shown? _____

3.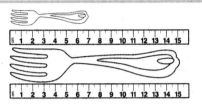

How much longer is one fork than the other? _____

4. Mariah has $3.99. After school, she spends $0.50 on a snack. How much money does Mariah have now?

_____

5. 113 + 215 =

6. 745 − 312 =

7. 8 + 4 = _____

2 + 10 = _____

9 + 8 = _____

8. Virginia stayed at an overnight camp for 14 days. She spent 10 nights in a log cabin and slept in the woods the other nights. How many nights did Virginia sleep in the woods? _____

9. Write the number 190 on the number line.

150   200

10. 74 + 33 = _____

91 − 42 = _____

 2.OA.1, 2.OA.2, 2.NBT.5, 2.NBT.7, 2.MD.4, 2.MD.5, 2.MD.6, 2.MD.7, 2.MD.8   CD-104591 • © Carson-Dellosa

Name_____

Day 1

532 + 213 =

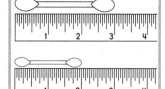

How many inches longer is one cotton swab than the other? _____

Carlos read 28 books in July and 30 books in August. How many more books did Carlos read during August than during July?

_____

9 + 7 = _____

11 – 6 = _____

9 – 4 = _____

Day 2

Arianna was paid 2 quarters, 3 dimes, 4 nickels, and 5 pennies for an apple pie she baked. How much money was she paid for her pie?

_____

Write the number 70 on the number line.

Is the number of full glasses even or odd? _____

786 – 231 =

Day 3

How many inches long is the piece of string? _____

Write the standard form for each expanded form.

900 + 50 + 9

_____

100 + 10 + 6

_____

---

270 + 21 =

Draw the hands on the clock to show 12:00.

Day 4

Pedro and Linden are playing a game. Linden has 75 squares. Pedro has 100. How many more squares does Pedro have?

_____

98 – 41 =

_____

78 + 15 =

_____

Add or subtract mentally.

499 – 10 =

_____

677 + 100 =

_____

What unit would you use to measure the length of the school building?

A. inches
B. meters
C. centimeters

Name_____

1. Write the number 60 on the number line.

40   100

2. Javon had $2.30 in his wallet. Draw one way to show what money Javon had in his wallet.

3. 561 + 238 =

4. Draw the hands on the clock to show 1:05.

5.

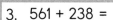

How many inches long is the watch?
_____

6. There are 64 students in the gym. There are 28 boys in the gym. How many girls are in the gym? _____

7. 7 – 6 = _____

   8 – 2 = _____

   5 + 12 = _____

8. 869 – 341 =

9.

How many inches longer is one rectangle than the other? _____

10. Write the standard form for each expanded form.

   600 + 50 = _____

   800 + 90 + 3 = _____

 2.OA.1, 2.OA.2, 2.NBT.3, 2.NBT.7, 2.MD.1, 2.MD.4, 2.MD.6, 2.MD.7, 2.MD.8   CD-104591 • © Carson-Dellosa

Name_____

Day 1

There are 52 dogs walking in Central Park. If 19 of the dogs are barking, how many of the dogs are not barking?

_____

16 + 41 + 21 + 6 =

Add or subtract mentally.

130 – 100 =

_____

55 + 10 =

_____

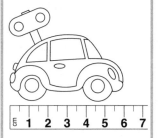

How long is the toy car? _____

Day 2

342 + 237 =

Courtney had some fabric. Becca gave her 12 more feet of fabric. Now, Courtney has 65 feet of fabric. How many feet of fabric did Courtney have to start with?

_____

Count by 5s.

245, _____,

255, _____,

265, _____

Warren has $3.78. He loans Trent $2.50. How much money does Warren have left?

_____

Day 3

Draw the hands on the clock to show 8:15.

41 – 20 =

_____

25 + 89 =

_____

Write an equation for the array.

_____

847 – 243 =

Day 4

5 + 6 = _____

1 + 12 = _____

6 – 2 = _____

Write <, >, or = to make the statements true.

130 ◯ 103

405 ◯ 450

90 ◯ 19

Owen and Jayla traveled 45 miles on Thursday and 58 miles on Friday. How many miles did Owen and Jayla travel in all?

_____

How much longer is one shoe than the other? _____

1.
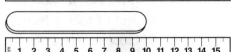

How much longer is one wooden craft stick than the other? _____

2. Draw the hands on the clock to show 3:25.

3. Armando has $2.29. His mom gives him $0.50 for making his bed. How much money does Armando have now?

_____

4. A cat climbed to the top of a 40-foot tree. A firefighter climbed up to rescue the cat. After 5 minutes, the firefighter had climbed 26 feet. How many more feet does the firefighter have to climb?

_____

5.

How long is the cookie? _____

6. 674 + 225 =

7. 12 – 2 = _____

   9 – 3 = _____

   11 – 5 = _____

8. Of the 74 cars parked in the parking lot, 17 are red. How many of the cars are not red? _____

9. 879 – 239 =

10. Count by 5s.

    555, 560, _____, _____,

    _____

Day 1

736 – 397 =

Divide the rectangle into four equal pieces.

Day 2

634 + 268 =

Room 2-B recycles 23 cans during May and 54 cans during June. How many more cans does Room 2-B recycle during June?

_____

Write the standard form for each expanded form.

600 + 20 + 6

_____

100 + 10 + 7

_____

Elijah sold his bike to Hunter. Hunter gave Elijah 3 one-dollar bills, 3 quarters, 5 dimes, 2 nickels, and 5 pennies. How much did Hunter pay Elijah for his bike? _____

Is the number of bees even or odd?

_____

Use the information below to fill in the line plot.

0 pets = 8 students
1 pet = 6 students
2 pets = 4 students

Number of Pets

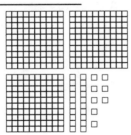

Day 3

7 – 5 = _____

10 – 3 = _____

10 – 1 = _____

Look at the base ten blocks. Write the number shown.

_____

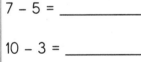

What time is shown?

_____

Day 4

272 + 13 =

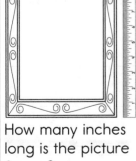

How many inches long is the picture frame? _____

What shape has 3 equal sides?

_____

Write <, >, or = to make the statements true.

456 ◯ 564

112 ◯ 112

32 ◯ 23

Cookies Baked for the Bake Sale

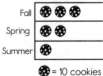

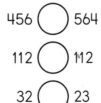

Fall
Spring
Summer

= 10 cookies

How many more cookies were baked for the fall sale than the spring sale? _____

Name_____

1. Divide the rectangle into two equal pieces.

2. Use the information below to fill in the line plot.

   0 servings = 0
   1 serving = 4
   2 servings = 3
   3 servings = 2
   4 servings = 1

   Servings of Fruit Eaten

   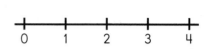

   0   1   2   3   4

3. How many pennies did the students spend altogether? _____

   Number of Pennies Spent

   Rebecca
   Jamie
   Sarah

   🅒 = 1 penny

4. Name the shape. _____

   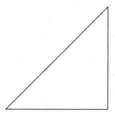

5. Anthony paid for his best friend's birthday present with 6 dimes, 3 one-dollar bills, and 3 quarters. How much money did Anthony spend? _____

6. 9 + 4 = _____

   2 + 6 = _____

   4 + 7 = _____

7. 987 – 489 =

8. 890 – 249 =

9. What time is shown? _____

   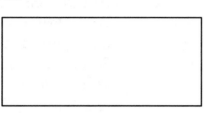

10. Write the expanded form for each number.

    451 _____

    206 _____

    210 _____

 2.OA.2, 2.NBT.3, 2.NBT.7, 2.MD.7, 2.MD.8, 2.MD.9, 2.MD.10, 2.G.1, 2.G.3   CD-104591 • © Carson-Dellosa

Name_____

Day 1

Use the information below to fill in the line plot.

3 letters = 1 student
4 letters = 4 students
5 letters = 4 students

Number of Letters in First Names

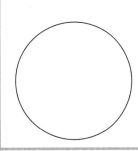

3   4   5

Which shape has 4 equal sides and 4 angles?

A. circle
B. square
C. rectangle

Divide the circle into three equal parts.

○

Day 2

If 68 children signed up to play lacrosse and 74 children signed up to play soccer, how many more children signed up to play soccer?

_____

Circle the digit in the tens place of each number.

74

456

31

190

123

---

6 + 10 = _____

8 + 2 = _____

2 + 1 = _____

Write the number for each number word.

six hundred fifty-five

_____

nine hundred twelve

_____

---

768 − 479 =

Day 3

Cans of Juice Sold

How many cans of juice were sold on Saturday and Sunday? _____

Count by 100s.

298, 398,

_____,

_____,

_____

Brad spent 3 quarters, 2 dimes, 1 nickel, and 5 pennies. How much money did he spend?

_____

Day 4

Add or subtract mentally.

870 + 100 =

_____

450 − 10 =

_____

Write an equation for the array.

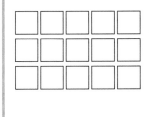

_____

---

493 − 277 =

---

94 − 86 =

_____

65 + 22 =

_____

Draw the hands on the clock to show 10:25.

---

1. 888 + 276 =

2. 385 – 269 =

3. 9 – 4 = _____

    4 – 1 = _____

    8 – 3 = _____

4. Use the information below to fill in the line plot.

    2 pencils = 4 students
    3 pencils = 2 students
    4 pencils = 5 students
    5 pencils = 0 students

    Number of Pencils in Students' Desks

    ```
    +----+----+----+----+
    2    3    4    5
    ```

5. Which shape has 5 sides and 5 angles?

    A. triangle
    B. circle
    C. pentagon

6. Draw the hands on the clock to show 6:30.

7. Holly earned 4 quarters, 6 dimes, 2 nickels, and 5 pennies for cleaning her room. How much money did Holly earn?

    _____

8.

    Trains Passing Through Station

    How many trains passed through the station at 7 am and 6 pm combined?

    _____

9. Circle the digit in the hundreds place of each number.

    318

    151

    220

    100

    45

10. Write the number for each number word.

    one hundred eleven _____

    four hundred thirty-six _____

2.OA.2, 2.NBT.1, 2.NBT.3, 2.NBT.7, 2.MD.7, 2.MD.8, 2.MD.9, 2.MD.10, 2.G.1   CD-104591 • © Carson-Dellosa

Name_____

Day 1

11 + 5 = _____

4 + 3 = _____

12 + 3 = _____

Charlotte had $4.05. She gave Abbie $2.00. How much money does Charlotte have left? _____

Write the numbers.

6 tens, 9 hundreds, 2 ones

_____

3 ones, 5 tens, 1 hundred

_____

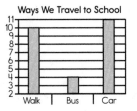

Ways We Travel to School

How many more students ride in a car than take the bus to school?

_____

Day 2

747 – 458 =

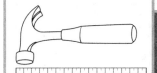

How long is the hammer?

_____

Is the number of bananas even or odd? _____

Use the information below to fill in the line plot.

12 chips = 2 cookies
13 chips = 7 cookies
14 chips = 1 cookie

Number of Chocolate Chips

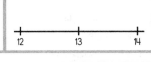
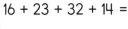

Day 3

732 – 299 =

Draw base ten blocks to show 697.

Mrs. Upton ordered 17 watermelons for the school picnic. If 11 of them were delivered on time and the rest of the watermelons were late, how many watermelons were delivered late?

_____

Name the shape that has 6 sides.

_____

Day 4

What time is shown?

_____

16 + 23 + 32 + 14 =

Count by 10s.

750, 760,

_____,

_____,

_____

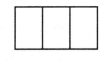

Describe how this rectangle is divided.

_____

1.

Describe how this circle is divided.
_____

2. Austin had $3.25. He bought a piece of bubble gum for $0.50. How much money does Austin have left? _____

3. $9 - 8 = $ _____

   $11 - 1 = $ _____

   $7 - 5 = $ _____

4. Name the shape that has 5 angles.

   _____

5. Use the information below to fill in the line plot.

   Number of Laps Run

   4 laps = 3 people
   5 laps = 5 people
   6 laps = 3 people

   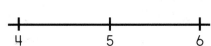

   4   5   6

6. $276 + 947 = $

7. $837 - 209 = $

8.

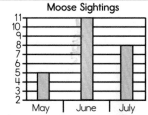

   How many more moose were sighted during June than May? _____

9. What time is shown? _____

10. There are 39 footballs and 45 basketballs in the gym. How many footballs and basketballs are there in all? _____

 2.OA.1, 2.NBT.7, 2.MD.7, 2.MD.8, 2.MD.9, 2.MD.10, 2.G.1, 2.G.3   CD-104591 • © Carson-Dellosa

Name_____

Day 1

Write the fraction for the shaded part of the shape.

_____

476 – 267 =

Day 2

Use the information below to fill in the line plot.

1 hour = 1 student
2 hours = 3 students
3 hours = 5 students

Hours Spent on Homework

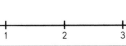

496 – 394 =

Janelle has $3.27. Draw one way to show the money that she has.

Write <, >, or = to make the statements true.

233 ◯ 214

960 ◯ 740

56 ◯ 58

At 5 years old, Heather was 38 inches tall. At 10 years old, she is now 54 inches tall. How much did Heather grow in 5 years?

_____

34 + 52 =

_____

86 – 21 =

_____

Day 3

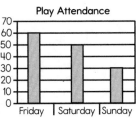

Play Attendance

What night did the most people attend the play?

_____

9 – 2 = _____

7 – 3 = _____

10 – 9 = _____

Day 4

Name the shape that has two sets of two equal sides.

_____

What time is shown?

_____

Which unit would you use to measure the length of your finger?

A. feet
B. yards
C. inches

Jenny is reading a book that is 98 pages long. She has read 47 pages so far. How many pages does Jenny have left to read?

_____

Draw an array for the equation.
3 + 3 + 3 = 9

Look at the base ten blocks. Write the number shown.

_____

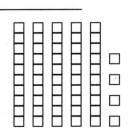

---

1. Use the information below to fill in the line plot.

6 years = 3 students   **Ages of Students in Our Class**
7 years = 9 students
8 years = 6 students

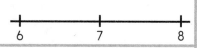

2. 557 + 323 =

3. 689 – 478 =

4. Benjamin has $4.65. Draw one way to show the money that he has.

5. What time is shown? _____

6.

Favorite Pets

How many students like fish more than cats? _____

7. Name the shape that has 6 congruent faces. _____

8. Write the fraction for the shaded part of the shape. _____

9. 5 + 3 = _____

   6 + 12 = _____

   8 + 6 = _____

10. 28 – 18 = _____

    89 – 53 = _____

Name_____

Day 1

Favorite Shapes

Square	☺
Circle	☺☺
Rectangle	☺

☺ = 5 children

How many children voted for their favorite shape?

_____

Count by 10s.

320, 330,

_____,

_____,

_____

---

5 + 9 = _____

9 + 11 = _____

12 + 4 = _____

Taylor paid for her new necklace with a five-dollar bill. If the necklace cost $3.48, how much change did Taylor get back?

_____

Day 2

Draw the hands on the clock to show 3:15.

Add or subtract mentally.

780 – 100 =

_____

430 + 10 =

_____

---

254 + 347 =

Catherine invited 38 people to her party. If 9 people were not able to come, how many people were able to come to her party? _____

Day 3

Shade in the circle to show the fraction $\frac{2}{4}$.

52 + 32 + 14 =

---

677 – 478 =

How many inches long is the notebook?

_____

Day 4

Name the shape.

_____

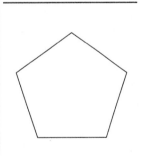

Is the number of owls even or odd?

_____

Use the information below to fill in the line plot.

1 mile = 6 students
2 miles = 4 students
3 miles = 5 students

Distance Lived from School

1   2   3

Write the standard form for each expanded form.

100 + 20 + 5

_____

400 + 90 + 5

_____

Name_____

---

1. Shade in the rectangle to show the fraction $\frac{1}{3}$.

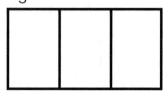

2. Draw the hand on the clock to show 7:35.

---

3. Adrian paid for his basketball with a five-dollar bill. If the basketball cost $4.17, how much change did Taylor get back?

_____

4. Write the standard form for each expanded form.

800 + 5 _____

600 + 40 + 7 _____

---

5. Name the shape. _____

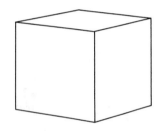

6. Use the information below to fill in the line plot.

5 inches = 4 students
6 inches = 4 students
7 inches = 7 students

Length of Pencils

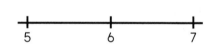

5   6   7

---

7. 376 – 187 =

8. 665 + 337 =

---

9. 4 + 11 = _____

9 + 5 = _____

11 – 3 = _____

10.

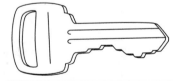

How many inches long is the key? _____

Name_____

Day 1

64 – 58 =

_____

87 + 46 =

_____

Amanda has 5 quarters in her change purse. She finds 5 nickels and 4 dimes on the sidewalk. How much money does she have now?

_____

Fish Caught

Mark |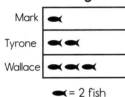
Tyrone |
Wallace |

= 2 fish

How many fish did Tyrone and Wallace catch altogether? _____

Write <, >, or = to make the statements true.

333 ◯ 303

191 ◯ 91

785 ◯ 758

Day 2

8 – 3 = _____

4 – 2 = _____

5 + 8 = _____

Name the polygon that has four angles. _____

Use the information below to fill in the line plot.

  3 feet = 9 people
  4 feet = 2 people
  5 feet = 3 people

Height of People's Windows

```
 +     +     +
 3     4     5
```

Write the number word for each number.

659

_____

974

_____

Day 3

493 + 229 =

There are 24 students in Room 2-L. Out of those 24, 15 of the students are wearing jeans. How many of the students are not wearing jeans?

_____

What time is shown?

_____

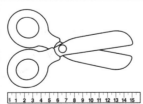

How long is the pair of scissors?

_____

Day 4

521 – 295 =

Add or subtract mentally.

350 + 100 =

_____

540 – 10 =

_____

Write the fraction for the shaded part of the shape.

_____

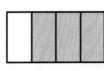

Count by 5s.

825, 830,

_____ ,

_____ ,

_____

1. Myra has $2.54. Her dad gives her $3.00 for washing the dishes after dinner. How much money does Myra have now?

   _____

2. 5 + 5 = _____

   11 + 3 = _____

   4 + 8 = _____

3. Colors of Cars in the Parking Lot

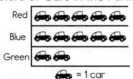

   Red
   Blue
   Green

   = 1 car

   Which color cars were present in the same amount in the parking lot? _____

4. What time is shown? _____

5. Write the fraction for the shaded part of the shape. _____

6. Use the information below to fill in the line plot.

   5 inches = 5 students   **Length of Students' Scissors**
   6 inches = 3 students
   7 inches = 2 students

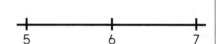

   5   6   7

7. 387 − 328 =

8. 988 + 748 =

9. Name the shape that has 6 angles.

   _____

10. Addison bakes 14 loaves of bread. She gives away 8 loaves of bread. How many loaves of bread does Addison have left?

    _____

 CD-104591 • © Carson-Dellosa

Name_____

Day 1

Name the shape.
Square

47 + 56 =
103

84 – 15 =
69

Day 2

Describe how the circle is divided.
thirds

Look at the base ten blocks. Write the number shown.
1 99

Olivia has 98 coins in her bank. She gives away 17 coins. How many coins does she have left?
81

98
17
81

Use the information below to fill in the line plot.
1 mile = 7 people
2 miles = 4 people
3 miles = 1 person

Distance Ridden on Bikes

Write the number that is 10 less than the number shown.

530 ____ 540

600 ____ 610

910 ____ 920

Books on a Shelf

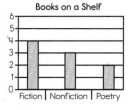

How many more fiction books than poetry books are there on the shelf?
2 books

Day 3

Deanna's total was $2.68. She paid with 3 one-dollar bills. How much change did Deanna get back? 32¢

Write the numbers.

6 hundreds, 8 tens, 4 ones
684

2 tens, 9 ones, 5 hundreds
529

Day 4

Draw the hands on the clock to show 6:15.

Count by 10s.

465, 475,
485
495
505

Krystal's jump rope measures 98 inches. Zack's jump rope measures 95 inches. How much longer is Krystal's jump rope than Zack's? 3 in

376 + 266 = 642

6 + 2 = 8

2 + 11 = 13

6 – 6 = 0

301 – 242 = 54

Name_____

1. Draw the hands on the clock to show 7:25.

2. Name the shape. _____

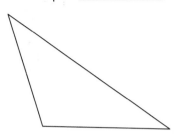

3. 8 – 6 = _____

   11 – 9 = _____

   7 + 11 = _____

4. 541 – 377 =

5. 249 + 233 =

6.

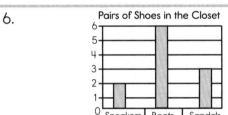

Pairs of Shoes in the Closet

How many pairs of shoes are in the closet? _____

7. Cameron paid with 6 quarters, 5 dimes, and 7 pennies. What was the total?

   _____

8. Use the information below to fill in the line plot.

   Length of Books on Shelf

   8 inches = 4
   9 inches = 2
   10 inches = 1

   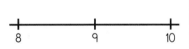

9. Describe how the circle is divided.

   _____

   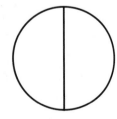

10. Write the numbers.

    5 ones, 6 hundreds, 2 tens

    _____

    8 tens, 9 ones, 2 hundreds

    _____

 2.OA.2, 2.NBT.3, 2.NBT.7, 2.MD.7, 2.MD.8, 2.MD.9, 2.MD.10, 2.G.1, 2.G.3   CD-104591 • © Carson-Dellosa

Name_____

Day 1

878 + 287 =

Use the information below to fill in the line plot.

1 inch = 7 students
2 inches = 5 students
3 inches = 4 students

Growth of Students in the Second Grade

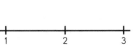

Day 2

471 − 382 =

Favorite
Ice Cream Flavors

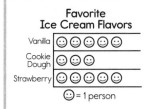

☺ = 1 person

How many people were surveyed to make this picture graph? _____

Nadia needs $5.00 to go on the field trip next week. She has already saved $3.64. How much more money does she need to save?

_____

Write the expanded form for each number.

27

_____

465

_____

89

_____

Color the cubes.

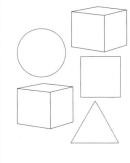

Forrest scored 12 points during his Monday night basketball game. On Tuesday night, he scored 22 points. How many points did Forrest score in all?

_____

Day 3

12 − 5 = _____

10 − 5 = _____

9 − 2 = _____

What time is shown?

_____

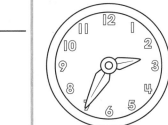

Day 4

60 − 10 =

_____

69 + 33 =

_____

Write the fraction for the shaded part of the shape.

_____

Draw base ten blocks to show 188.

Is the number of stars even or odd?

_____

Write <, >, or = to make the statements true.

226 ◯ 436

954 ◯ 954

310 ◯ 31

45 + 16 + 10 + 28 =

Name_____

1. Color the shapes with 4 equal sides.

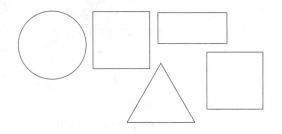

2. Garrick needed $9.50 to go to the movies. His dad gave him $3.25, and his mom gave him $2.75. How much more money does Garrick need to go to the movies? _____

3. Write the fraction for the shaded part of the shape. _____

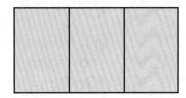

4. $5 - 3 =$ _____

$10 - 4 =$ _____

$7 - 3 =$ _____

5.

Animals in the Zoo

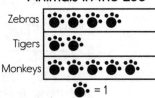

How many monkeys and tigers were there at the zoo? _____

6. What time is shown? _____

7. $727 - 419 =$

8. $436 + 296 =$

9. Use the information below to fill in the line plot.

Length of Girls' Hair

10 inches = 2 girls
11 inches = 3 girls
12 inches = 6 girls

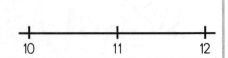

10. There are 19 trees in Lynn's front yard and 27 trees in her backyard. How many total trees are there in Lynn's front yard and backyard? _____

Name_____

Day 1

Show two different ways to divide the rectangles into thirds.

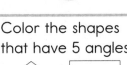

348 + 948 =

Day 1 / top middle

Write the number for each number word.

two hundred seven

_____

one hundred eighteen

_____

Use the information below to fill in the line plot.

7 cm = 5 crayons
8 cm = 3 crayons
9 cm = 7 crayons

Length of Crayons

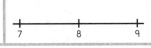

```
+-------+-------+-------+
7       8       9
```

848 – 399 =

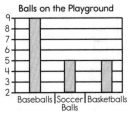

What kinds of balls were present in equal amounts on the playground?

_____

Day 2

A total of 38 people are waiting for a bus to take them to Atlanta. Later, 5 more people arrive to wait for the bus. How many people are waiting for the bus now?

_____

How long is the watch? _____

Day 3

What time is shown?

_____

Color the shapes that have 5 angles.

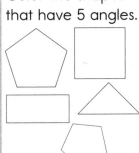

Draw an array for the equation.

5 + 5 + 5 + 5 + 5 = 25

27 + 42 =

_____

49 – 37 =

_____

There are 3 one-dollar bills, 7 quarters, 5 dimes, 3 nickels, and 10 pennies in a jar. How much money is in the jar?

_____

1 + 11 = _____

12 + 9 = _____

10 + 3 = _____

Day 4

Use the following clues to write a 3-digit number.

The digit in the tens place is 3. The digit in the hundreds place is greater than 5 and less than 7. The only remaining digit is 0.

_____

Add or subtract mentally.

29 + 10 =

_____

255 – 100 =

_____

1. Gregory saved 4 one-dollar bills, 8 quarters, 10 nickels, and 24 pennies in a shoe box. How much money does Gregory have? _____

2. What time is shown? _____

3. Cookies in the Jar

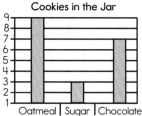

How many chocolate and sugar cookies are there in the cookie jar? _____

4. Color the shapes that have 6 sides.

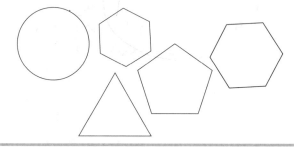

5. Show two different ways to divide the circles into halves.

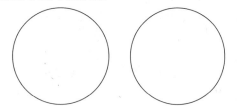

6. Use the information below to fill in the line plot.

Length of Lunchboxes

25 cm = 3 students
26 cm = 5 students
27 cm = 9 students

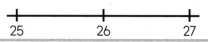

7. 8 + 11 = _____

   5 – 2 = _____

   7 – 6 = _____

8. Use the following clues to write a 3-digit number.

   The digits in this number are 6, 5, and 2.
   The digit in the ones place is greater than 1, but less than 4.
   The largest digit belongs in the tens place.

   _____

9. 498 + 439 =

10. 847 – 358 =

Name_____

Day 1

Write the fraction for the shaded part of the shape.

_____

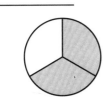

94 – 66 =

_____

87 + 45 =

_____

Write the number for each number word.

four hundred thirteen

_____

three hundred sixty

_____

Jackie jumps rope for 31 minutes Saturday and 27 minutes Sunday. How many more minutes does Jackie jump rope on Saturday than Sunday?

_____

Day 2

Draw the hands on the clock to show 11:45.

Is the number of baseballs even or odd? _____

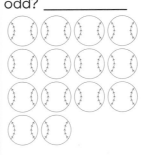

Look at the base ten blocks. Write the number shown.

_____

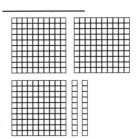

Use the information below to fill in the line plot.

16 inches = 3 sticks
17 inches = 7 sticks
18 inches = 4 sticks

Length of Sticks on the Playground

Day 3

Colors of Boats on the Lake

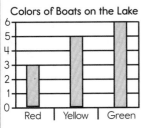

How many more yellow boats than red boats were on the lake? _____

Count by 10s.

916, 926,

_____,

_____,

_____

502 – 321 =

12 – 1 = _____

6 + 4 = _____

9 + 10 = _____

Day 4

Name the shape.

_____

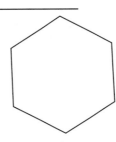

Write <, >, or = to make the statements true.

115 254

333 ◯ 222

54 ◯ 540

477 + 298 =

Iesha has $5.65 saved. Ansley has $4.35 saved. How much more money does Iesha have?

_____

Name_____

---

1. Name the shape. _____

2. Use the information below to fill in the line plot.

   Length of Ice-Cream Cones

   19 inches = 4 cones
   20 inches = 2 cones
   21 inches = 1 cone

   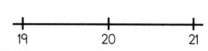

---

3. Pablo scored 14 goals in September, 8 goals in October, and 12 goals in November. How many more goals did Patrick score in September than October? _____

4. Darius spent $4.35 at the arcade. Cheryl spent $3.45 at the arcade. How much more money did Darius spend than Cheryl? _____

---

5. Draw the hands on the clock to show 2:25.

   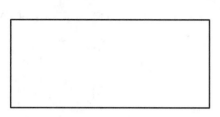

6. Write the fraction for the shaded part of the shape. _____

   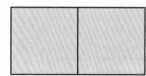

---

7. 6 – 3 = _____

   11 – 10 = _____

   2 – 2 = _____

8. 396 + 298 =

---

9. 704 – 597 =

10. Count by 10s.
    54, 64, _____, _____,

    _____

 2.OA.1, 2.OA.2, 2.NBT.2, 2.NBT.7, 2.MD.7, 2.MD.8, 2.MD.9, 2.G.1, 2.G.3   CD-104591 • © Carson-Dellosa

Answer Key

Page 9
Day 1: 24; ; 5 animals; 5;
Day 2: 17 – 7 = 10; B; C; 7, 8, 9; **Day 3:** B; B; 8, 10, 4; 7; **Day 4:** Evan; 12; A; 45

Page 10
1. 10; 2. 5; 3. C; 4. 8 crayons; 5. C; 6. B; 7. 26; 8. B; 9. 10 cents; 10. zebras

Page 11
Day 1: 31; ; 12 squirrels; 7; **Day 2:** 58; C; B; even; **Day 3:** C; 5 cm; 1, 3, 5; 8; **Day 4:** Sean; 25; <; B

Page 12
1. 11; 2. 8; 3. odd; 4. B; 5. 11, 6, 8; 6. B; 7. 56; 8. Irene; 9. ; 10. >

Page 13
Day 1: ; 7; 7 apples; **Day 2:** 37; B; 12 cents; odd; **Day 3:** 3; 1 cm; 3; B; **Day 4:** 58; <; C; bananas and oranges

Page 14
1. 1; 2. 5; 3. <; 4. 8 – 4 = 4 cookies; 5. C; 6. A; 7. ; 8. ; 9. 5 cents; 10. 8

Page 15
Day 1: ; ; 5; 3 – 2 = 1 kitten; **Day 2:** 61; A; 8:00; 7; **Day 3:** 7; 6 cm; 21; 22; **Day 4:** even; 24 cents; 10; Noah

Page 16
1. 8 inches; 2. ; 3. 5:00; 4. Kevin; 5. odd; 6. 8 – 5 = 3 marbles; 7. 18; 8. 6; 9. 3; 10. 7

Page 17
Day 1: four, ten, seven; Answers will vary; 4 – 1 = 3 lollipops; 5, 3, 6; **Day 2:** 11:00; 20, 25, 30; 49; <; **Day 3:** >; 12 cents; 10; Valerie; **Day 4:** B; 1 foot; 7, 4, 8; 25, 26, 27, 28

Page 18
1. 4:00; 2. ; 3. 35, 40, 45; 4. 8 – 3 = 5 cars; 5. 34, 36; 6. fourteen, nine, one; 7. 5; 8. 8; 9. <; 10. 57

Page 19
Day 1: 64; Answers will vary; 2 + 5 + 1 = 8 writing tools; 10, 7, 5; **Day 2:** 41; 40, 50, 60; 16 cents; 45; **Day 3:** odd; 6:00; four, six, eight; 7, 0, 12; **Day 4:** 6 scoops; <, <, =; 62, 34, 30; 2

Page 20
1. 9; 2. 0; 3. 58; 4. 3 + 2 = 5 beads; 5. 13 cents; 6. >, >, <; 7. 7:00; 8. 36; 9. six, two, four; 10. even, 6 + 6 = 12

Page 21
Day 1: 51; ; 6 – 2 = 4 goldfish; 1, 11, 5; **Day 2:** 16; 6 cents; 1:00; 13; **Day 3:** 28, 35, 12; 7 cm; 12, 9, 14; 2, 10, 10; **Day 4:** 5 pictures; 7 grapes; <; odd

Page 22
1. 9; 2. 4; 3. 35 cents; 4. 5 – 3 = 2 pens;
5. 4:00; 6. 30, 51, 46; 7. 19; 8. ◯ ; 9. 54 cents; 10. 1 student

Page 23
Day 1: 68; ☐☐☐ ; 15 hours; 4, 24;
Day 2: 11 cupcakes; 76; 9:00; 25, 27, 20;
Day 3: 60, 65, 70; 30; =, <, >; 2, 22;
Day 4: 13 puppies; 7 tens, 2 ones; 50, 11, 8; 43 cents

Page 24
1. 22; 2. 21; 3. 45, 50, 55; 4. 14 – 4 = 10 tennis balls; 5. 48; 6. 9 days; 7. 17, 13, 15; 8. A;
9. 3:30; 10. 8 tens, 7 ones

Page 25
Day 1: 89, 73, 48; hexagon; 30 items of clothing; 12, 14, 10; **Day 2:** 59; even; 8:30; 60, 70, 80; **Day 3:** <, >, >; 42 cents; 96; 30, 2; **Day 4:** 27 people; 21, 23, 11; 16 + 14 = 30; 87

Page 26
1. 6; 2. 22; 3. 10; 4. >, >, >; 5. 41, 29, 15; 6. 80, 90, 100; 7. 10:30; 8. even; 9. 80 cents; 10. 88

Page 27
Day 1: 80 + 3; 5; 28 – 16 = 12 flowers; 11, 20; **Day 2:** 100; 14 – 8 = 6 rocks; 12 cents; 70, 75, 80; **Day 3:** >, <, >; even; 70; 19, 12; **Day 4:** 7:30; 26, 53, 32; 11 goldfish; 2 eggs

Page 28
1. 20; 2. 19; 3. 60, 65, 70; 4. 49; 5. 18 – 4 = 14 bones; 6. blue; 7. 15, 17, 26; 8. 5:30;
9. >, <; 10. even

Page 29
Day 1: 90 + 8; 6; 2 days; 28, 20, 7;
Day 2: 1, 0, 5; even; 55 cents; 400, 500, 600; **Day 3:** thirteen, twenty-four, forty-three; 75; ⊢—┼—┼—⊢ (0, 10, 15, 20); 5:05;
Day 4: 34 students; 5 cents; >, >, =; 7, 9, 6

Page 30
1. 12 + 6 = 18 campers; 2. 50 + 4, 70 + 8;
3. 1, 2, 1; 4. 6:15; 5. 50 cents; 6. seventeen, twenty-one, sixty-one; 7. 25, 34, 54; 8. 600, 700, 800; 9. 59; 10. odd

Page 31
Day 1: 432, 204; square; 4 miles; 67, 78;
Day 2: 120, 125, 130; Philip; 3:20; 204;
Day 3: 60, 336, 154; odd; >, <, <; 29 piles;
Day 4: 10, 14, 11; 11 – 4 = 7 stars; 16, 21, 19; B

Page 32
1. 156; 2. 79; 3. 10 cupcakes; 4. C; 5. 532;
6. 240, 245, 250; 7. 426, 555, 300; 8. 7, 8, 9;
9. 7:45; 10. odd

Page 33
Day 1: >; 8; 30 hours; 8, 15, 10; **Day 2:** A; 370, 380, 390; 11:00; 51, 79; **Day 3:** Answers will vary; 342; 300 + 80 + 9; 440, 280, 100;
Day 4: 3 cm; odd; thirty-one, fifty-five, seventy-two; 6, 15, 9

Page 34
1. 31; 2. 94; 3. 9:00; 4. Answers will vary;
5. A; 6. 550, 580, 590; 7. 12, 10, 9; 8. 35; 9. 7;
10. 2 grandchildren

Page 35
Day 1: 3 bubble wands; 520, 620, 720; 94; 10, 12, 15; **Day 2:** 45, 88, 93; <, <; 12:30; B; **Day 3:** Answers will vary; 35; even; 33; **Day 4:** 13 – 4 = 9 burgers;

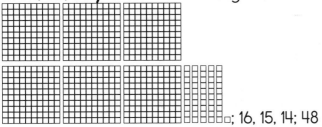

; 16, 15, 14; 48

Page 36
1. 13, 7, 15; 2. C; 3. 5 pages; 4. 25; 5. 710, 810, 910; 6. >, <; 7. Answers will vary;

8. ;
9. 10:30; 10. 56

Page 37
Day 1: 10, 10, 9; 300; 591, 442, 947; 3 baskets; **Day 2:** $1.05; 370, 375, 380; 9 + 3 = 12 balloons; 50; **Day 3:** 12:00; 5 + 5 = 10 or 2 + 2 + 2 + 2 + 2 = 10; thirty,

sixty-one, seventy-three; 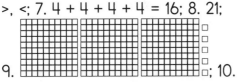; **Day 4:**

; 4 monkeys; 34; >, <, =

Page 38
1. 6:05; 2. 83; 3. 5; 4. 1, 6, 2; 5. 90 cents; 6. <, >, <; 7. 4 + 4 + 4 + 4 = 16; 8. 21;

9. ; 10.

Page 39
Day 1: ; <, >, <; 120, 630, 890; 12, 14, 16; **Day 2:** Answers will vary; 130; ; 67; **Day 3:** 30 frames; 305, 923; 360, 370; 35; **Day 4:** 3 + 3 + 3 = 9; 12 roses; 40 cents; 67

Page 40
1. 6, 8, 7; 2. 99; 3. 42; 4. 6 red beads;

5. Answers will vary; 6. ; 7. 1 + 1 + 1 + 1 + 1 = 5; 8. <, >; 9. 820, 830; 10. 747, 207

Page 41
Day 1: 200 + 30, 500 + 70 + 3; Answers will vary; 555, 148, 113; 16 alarm clocks;

Day 2: ; 545, 745; 800, 8, 80; eighteen, sixty-four, five; **Day 3:** 55; 1, 3, 4; 84; <, >, >; **Day 4:** 7 sweaters; 33; 10, 12, 11;

Page 42
1. Answers will vary; 2. 65; 3. 15; 4. 69; 5. 32

bananas; 6. 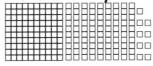; 7. 16, 2; 8. 30, 30, 3; 9. <, <, >; 10. 100 + 7, 300 + 20

Answer Key

Page 43

Day 1: Answers will vary; 66; 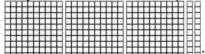; 24; **Day 2:** 9; 143; 645, 360; 815, 915 **Day 3:** 3 + 3 + 3 = 9; ; 22 eggs; 77; **Day 4:** ; >, <, <; 57 cents; 12, 8, 15

Page 44

1. 66; 2. 34; 3. 1, 5; 4. 1 + 1 + 1 + 1 = 4;

5. ; 6. 85 cents; 7. 35 magazines; 8. 72; 9. 320, 420, 520;

10.

Page 45

Day 1: 13; 86; ; 49; **Day 2:** 0, 3, 8;

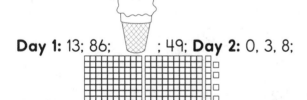

5 books; ; 5 – 2 = 3 cows; **Day 3:** 14 girls; 615, 620, 625; 15, 9, 9; $1.05; **Day 4:** 96; >, <, =; Answers will vary; 1:00

Page 46

1. Answers will vary; 2. 55 cents; 3. 13, 9, 9; 4. 89; 5. 33; 6. 4:30; 7. 18 books; 8. 79; 9. >, <, >; 10. 135, 140, 145

Page 47

Day 1: 8:30; 450, 460, 470; 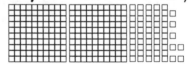; 14, 11, 12; **Day 2:** Answers will vary; 251; Answers will vary; 5, 4, 0; **Day 3:** 22; three hundred, one hundred fifty-two; 404, 25, 60; 22 balls; **Day 4:** 99; 400 + 5; 2 butterflies; 96

Page 48

1. Answers will vary; 2. Answers will vary;

3. 7:30; 4. 15, 13, 8; 5. 37; 6. 89; 7. ; 8. A; 9. 40 students; 10. 64

Page 49

Day 1: 3, 2, 17; 34, 37; <, >, <; 86;

Day 2: 9:30; 76, 99; ; 740, 750, 760; **Day 3:** Answers will vary; 8 pencils; 77; two hundred ten, six hundred three; **Day 4:** Answers will vary; 3; 9 cookies;

Page 50

1. 15; 2. 13, 16, 3; 3. 11:00; 4. Answers will vary; 5. 88, 91; 6. 16 cards; 7. Answers will vary; 8. 820, 830; 9. 69; 10. four hundred fifteen, one hundred twelve

Page 51

Day 1: 8 stamps; Answers will vary; 356, 721; 4 cm; **Day 2:** 14, 12, 5; 136, 21; 96; 69 feet; **Day 3:** 799; >, <, >; 533; ; **Day 4:** A; 470, 570, 670; 61 books; 5:45

Page 52
1. 3:20; 2. ; 3. 30 cm;
4. 2 cm; 5. 889; 6. 216; 7. 112, 52; 8. 10, 10, 9;
9. 14 papers; 10. >, >, <

Page 53
Day 1: ; 2, 5, 3; 73; 550;
Day 2: 7 cm; 254; Answers will vary; 25;
Day 3: 16 inches; ; Answers will vary;
8 shirts; **Day 4:** 2 + 2 + 2 + 2 = 8 or
4 + 4 = 8; 14, 69; 230, 250, 260;

Page 54
1. 432; 2. 147; 3. 2, 9, 0;
4. ; 5. 63 yards; 6. 1 inch;
7. ; 8. 12 games; 9. Answers will vary;
10. 3 inches

Page 55
Day 1: 2 cm; 517, 136; ;
234; **Day 2:** 6:35; 6, 98; C; $2.65; **Day 3:**
8 cm; 97; 28 fish; 20, 19, 20; **Day 4:** 799; >,
=, <; Answers will vary; 7 feet

Page 56
1. 143, 37; 2. 15, 22, 6; 3. 9:10; 4. $5.00;
5. 11; 6. 6 cm; 7. 4 inches; 8. 79 inches;
9. 11 minutes; 10. 122

Page 57
Day 1: 8; >, <, >; 9 inches; 11; **Day 2:** 5:55;
even; 2 cm; 18, 10, 6; **Day 3:** 500; three
hundred fifty-four, nine hundred two;
22 blocks; 84, 79; **Day 4:** 56; Answers will
vary; C; 60 cents

Page 58
1. 3 inches; 2. 8 inches; 3. 14; 4. centimeters;
5. $3.39; 6. 6, 1, 7; 7. 6:00; 8. 100; 9. 465;
10. odd

Page 59
Day 1: 11, 2, 1; 425; 396; 79; **Day 2:** 3 cm;
750, 850, 950; 330, 520; 648; **Day 3:**
; 90, 43; 102; $6.50;
Day 4: B; 8:40; >, <, <; 8 inches

Page 60
1. $0.80; 2. 694; 3. 62; 4. 3 cm; 5. 5, 4, 19;
6. 9:05; 7. feet; 8. 15 inches; 9. 278; 10. 490, 68

Page 61
Day 1: $1.00; 1 inch; 100, 56; 18, 11, 16;
Day 2: 14; ; 427, 909;
967; **Day 3:** 12 inches; A; odd; 230; **Day 4:**
1 inch; 35; 129;

Page 62
1. 104; 2. $0.18; 3. 10, 13, 3; 4. 10 inches;
5. ; 6. 105; 7. 696; 8. 166; 9. 1 inch;
10. 2 feet

Page 63
Day 1: 4:45; C; <, >, =; 111; **Day 2:** $0.23;
; 360, 550; 999;
Day 3: 25; four hundred twenty-two,
seventy-two; 2 cm; 0, 1, 11; **Day 4:** 11 cm;
29, 88; 291; 36 inches

Page 64
1. 88 inches; 2. 10:35; 3. 8 cm; 4. $3.49;
5. 328; 6. 433; 7. 12, 12, 17; 8. 4;
9. ; 107, 49

Page 65

Day 1: 745; 1 inch; 2; 16, 5, 5; **Day 2:** $1.05;

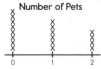 ; even; 555; **Day 3:**

9 inches; 959, 116; 291; ; **Day 4:** 25;
57, 93; 489, 777; B

Page 66

1. ; 2. Answers will vary;

3. 799; 4. ; 5. 10 inches; 6. 36; 7. 1, 6,
17; 8. 528; 9. 3 inches; 10. 650, 893

Page 67

Day 1: 33; 84; 30, 65; 6 cm; **Day 2:** 579;

53 feet; 250, 260, 270; $1.28; **Day 3:** ;
21, 114; Answers will vary; 604; **Day 4:** 11, 13,
4; >, <. >; 103 miles, 6 cm

Page 68

1. 3 cm; 2. ; 3. $2.79; 4. 14 feet;
5. 8 cm; 6. 899; 7. 10, 6, 6; 8. 57; 9. 640;
10. 565, 570, 575

Page 69

Day 1: 339; Answers will vary; 626;
117; $4.40; **Day 2:** 902; 31 cans; even;

Number of Pets

; **Day 3:** 2, 7, 9; 328; 9
inches; triangle; **Day 4:** 7:50; 285; <, =, >; 10

Page 70

Servings of Fruit Eaten Yesterday

1. ; 2.  ; 3. 15; 4.
triangle; 5. $4.35; 6. 13, 8, 11; 7. 498; 8. 641;
9. 11:15; 10. 400 + 50 + 1, 200 + 6, 200 + 10

Page 71

Number of Letters in First Names

Day 1: ; B; 7, 5, 3, 9, 2; 16, 10, 3;

Day 2: 6; 655, 912; 289; **Day 3:** 70;
498, 598, 698; Answers will vary; 216;

Day 4: $1.05; 970, 440; 8, 87;

Page 72

Number of Pencils
in Students' Desks

1. 1,164; 2. 116; 3. 5, 3, 5; 4. ;

5. C; 6. ; 7. $1.75; 8. 37; 9. 3, 1, 2, 1, 0;
10. 111, 436

Page 73

Day 1: 16, 7, 15; $2.05; 962, 153; 7 students;

Number of Chocolate Chips

Day 2: 289; 15 cm; even; 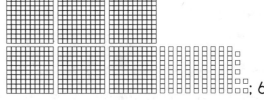 ;
Day 3: 433;

; 6;
hexagon; **Day 4:** 1:40; 85; 770, 780, 790;
thirds

CD-104591 • © Carson-Dellosa

Page 74

1. fourths; 2. $2.75; 3. 1, 10, 2; 4. pentagon;

Number of Laps Run

5. 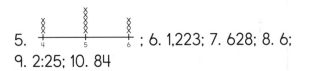 ; 6. 1,223; 7. 628; 8. 6;
9. 2:25; 10. 84

Page 75

Day 1: $\frac{1}{2}$; 209; Answers will vary; >, >, <;

Hours Spent on Homework

Day 2: 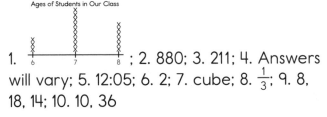 ; 102; 16 inches; 86,
65; **Day 3:** Friday; 7, 4, 1; C; 51; **Day 4:**
rectangle; 8:05; Answers will vary; 54

Page 76

Ages of Students in Our Class

1. ; 2. 880; 3. 211; 4. Answers
will vary; 5. 12:05; 6. 2; 7. cube; 8. $\frac{1}{3}$; 9. 8,
18, 14; 10. 10, 36

Page 77

Day 1: 20 children; 340, 350, 360; 14, 20,

16; $1.52; **Day 2:** ; 680, 440; 601; 29

people; **Day 3:** ; 98; 199; 7 inches;

Distance Lived from School

Day 4: pentagon; odd; ; 125,
495

Page 78

1. ; 2. ; 3. $0.83; 4. 805, 647;

Length of Pencils

5. cube; 6. ; 7. 189; 8. 1,002;
9. 15, 14, 8; 10. 5 inches

Page 79

Day 1: 6, 133; $1.90; 10 fish; >, >, >; **Day 2:**

Height of People's Windows

5, 2, 13 quadrilaterals; ; six
hundred fifty-nine, nine hundred seventy-
four; **Day 3:** 722; 9 students; 7:50; 15 cm;
Day 4: 226; 450, 530; $\frac{3}{4}$; 835, 840, 845

Page 80

1. $5.54; 2. 10, 14, 12; 3. red and blue; 4. 1:05;

Length of Students' Scissors

5. $\frac{1}{2}$; 6. ; 7. 59; 8. 1,736;
9. hexagon; 10. 6 loaves

Page 81

Day 1: square; 103, 69; 81 coins;

Distance Ridden on Bikes

; **Day 2:** thirds; 199; 530,
600, 910; 2; **Day 3:** $0.32; 684, 529; 3

inches; 642; **Day 4:** ; 485, 495, 505;
8, 13, 0; 59

Answer Key

Page 82

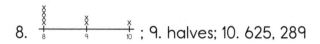

1. ; 2. triangle; 3. 2, 2, 18; 4. 164; 5. 482; 6. 11 pairs of shoes; 7. $2.07;

Length of Books on Shelf

8.  ; 9. halves; 10. 625, 289

Page 83

Growth of Students in the Second Grade

Day 1: 1,165; ; $1.36; 20 + 7, 400 + 60 + 5, 80 + 9; **Day 2:** 89; 13 people;

; 34 points; **Day 3:** 7, 5, 7;

2:35; ; odd; **Day 4:** 50, 102; $\frac{4}{4}$; <, =, >; 99

Page 84

1. ; 2. $3.50; 3. $\frac{3}{3}$; 4. 2, 6, 4; 5. 7 monkeys and tigers; 6. 7:55; 7. 308; 8. 732;

Length of Girls' Hair

9. ; 10. 46 trees

Page 85

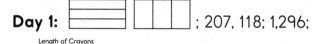

Day 1: ; 207, 118; 1,296;

Length of Crayons

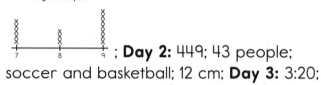 ; **Day 2:** 449; 43 people; soccer and basketball; 12 cm; **Day 3:** 3:20;

Answers will vary; 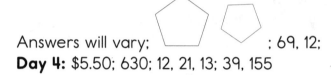 ; 69, 12; **Day 4:** $5.50; 630; 12, 21, 13; 39, 155

Page 86

1. $6.74; 2. 9:45; 3. 10 cookies;

4. 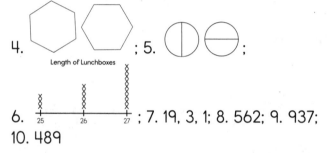 ; 5. ;

Length of Lunchboxes

6. 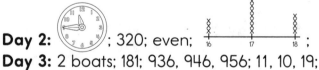 ; 7. 19, 3, 1; 8. 562; 9. 937; 10. 489

Page 87

Day 1: $\frac{2}{3}$; 413, 360; 28, 132; 4 minutes;

Length of Sticks on the Playground

Day 2: ; 320; even; ; **Day 3:** 2 boats; 181; 936, 946, 956; 11, 10, 19; **Day 4:** hexagon; 775; <, >, <; $1.30

Page 88

Length of Ice-Cream Cones

1. rectangle; 2. 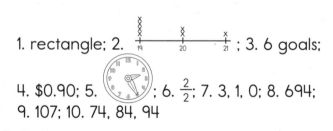 ; 3. 6 goals;

4. $0.90; 5. ; 6. $\frac{2}{2}$; 7. 3, 1, 0; 8. 694; 9. 107; 10. 74, 84, 94

CD-104591 • © Carson-Dellosa